MW00613803

# AFTER THE FUNERAL

## A Practical Memoir for Administering Your Loved One's Estate

# AFTER THE FUNERAL

## A Practical Memoir for Administering Your Loved One's Estate

### Eileen Moynahan

**Niche Pressworks**

Indianapolis

After the Funeral: A Practical Memoir for Administering Your Loved One's Estate
ISBN 978-1-946533-42-5 (Paperback)
ISBN 978-1-946533-41-8 (Ebook)

Copyright © 2019 by Eileen Moynahan

All rights reserved. No part of this book may be used or reproduced in any manner whatsoever without prior written consent of the author, except as provided by the United States of America copyright law.

This book is not meant to serve as legal advice. For legal advice, consult an attorney licensed to practice in your state.

Illustrations by Quincy Sutton; find him at Upwork.com.

Author photograph by Juliet Foster; find her at JFosterImagery.com.

For permission to reprint portions of this content or bulk purchases, contact Eileen Moynahan at Eileen@LegacyEstateOrganizing.com.

Published by Niche Pressworks, Indianapolis, IN

http://NichePressworks.com

Printed in the United States of America

# DEDICATION

To my parents, Mary Theresa McEvoy Moynahan and Bartholomew John Moynahan, who continue to inspire me every day, and in every way, of my life.

It is my hope that this book serves as a humble tribute to the people you were and the good you gave.

# ACKNOWLEDGEMENTS

I wish to thank hundreds of people for making this book—and my business—a reality. But I'll focus on the very top of the list.

Thank you to my brother Thomas Moynahan and my sister Theresa Moynahan for their love and support but more specifically for their endless supply of class in the days, weeks, and months following our parents' deaths. You both made the whole estate process so much easier by your actions. I would also like to take this opportunity to apologize for that day we removed the carpeting and padding at Mom and Dad's house. Who knew there was a specific device designed to remove carpet staples?? Your nails will grow back someday.

*Muchísimas gracias* to the Diaz and Rosa families, who adopted me when I became orphaned and who continue to include me in all things family.

Thank you to my parents' estate attorney, Christopher Rohde of Rohde Law Group, Caldwell, New Jersey, for your guidance, kindness, and professionalism then and your ongoing support now as I apply some of the lessons you taught me during this new season of my life.

A special thanks to Nicole Gebhardt and Kim Han at Niche Pressworks, who gave me the road map, served as my pit crew, and essentially oiled the gears throughout this writing and publishing process. I would still be sitting in front of a pile of index cards were it not for you.

Thank you to the Suffern Free Library in Suffern, New York, for providing a calm, quiet, and comfortable setting in which I wrote 90% of this book, away from the temptations of doing laundry, watching HGTV, and studying squirrels—because no one procrastinates better than a writer!

Last but not least, I offer the utmost love and gratitude to my wonderful husband Edwin Diaz, who stood beside me, behind me, and everywhere in between during the worst days of my life ... proving that Mary and Bart chose their son-in-law well. So glad that you agreed to a drink (in lieu of going home to do laundry) that Friday night in September 2007. I am constantly amazed that you continue to love me despite my extensive character flaws. *Tu eres mi corazón, mi vida, mi media-naranja, mi sol y luna. Te adoro, Eddie.*

# CONTENTS

# PREFACE

*With my mother's death, all settled happiness, all that was tranquil and reliable, disappeared from my life. There was to be much fun, many pleasures, many stabs of Joy; but no more of the old security. It was sea and islands now; the great continent had sunk like Atlantis.*

– C.S. LEWIS

## May 5, 2012

I felt a general sense of unease that entire Saturday, despite the fact that we were enjoying beautiful spring weather and my morning chores had gone well. I had hit the bank, the grocery store, and a home-goods store to purchase a selection of annuals for the yard. My husband Eddie had left that morning to drive upstate to pick up his son from college. It was two hours each way. Factoring in the loading and unloading of the car, he expected to be home by dinnertime.

Maybe I was restless because my Uncle Jim had passed away three days before. He had been battling health challenges for some time, so while his death was not unexpected, it was still something we were all processing. My parents had been trying to figure out the best way to get to the funeral in Erie, Pennsylvania since they had received the news. We had many conversations about who could go from our family and how we would get there.

My parents didn't really want to drive all that way, but they were foiled in their attempt to fly (there were no direct flights, and even connecting flights were outrageously priced) or to take a train or bus. In the end, they decided to make the seven-hour drive to Erie and had departed that Saturday morning after my mother's usual hair appointment. My uncle's wake was scheduled for Sunday and his funeral the following day.

As I thought about these details, I recalled the last time I had seen my Uncle Jim, at my wedding 18 months prior. He had been in good health and good humor, and all three of his adult children had been able to join my aunt and him at the wedding. We had a humorous moment prior to the wedding itself.

Eddie and I had taken refuge inside the venue so that everyone wouldn't see us in our finery before the ceremony. My uncle, a handsome man with that great clipped speech pattern you hear in 1930s movies and an unceasingly dry wit, came into the entrance of the building with my Aunt Maggie. The parking valets were outside the doors, taking cars from our wedding guests as they showed up for the ceremony. As I stood there in my wedding gown, veil on, holding my gorgeous, white-orchid bouquet, my uncle took one look at me and said, "Geez, they've got you parking cars as well??"

I had a busy work week coming up, as did Eddie, so I had gone back and forth for the past two days debating whether to drive out to Erie on Sunday and back on Monday after the funeral repast. My mother worried about me making the long drive by myself and tried to dissuade me from going. I initially had considered riding with my parents, but they were staying Saturday through Tuesday, which was much longer than I could spend out there. I was going over options in my head as I planted a window box, put pansies along a border, and cleaned up afterwards. I was still undecided as I headed inside for lunch.

The next sequence of events is understandably muddled in my mind. I remember standing in the kitchen and looking out the wall of windows to see a police cruiser in my driveway. Being the quintessential, law-abiding nerd that I am (and with my husband and I both employed in law enforcement), I was surprised and perplexed. I couldn't remember doing anything even remotely illegal and couldn't work out in my head why two police officers would be approaching our patio.

All at once, the realization hit me. Someone I loved was seriously injured or dead, and these officers had the unwelcome task of notifying me as next of kin.

I immediately presumed it was Eddie. He is a senior investigator with the New York State Police (NYSP), and he was on the road that day heading to Albany. His address (our address) would be on his license, and if the trooper who came upon the accident had run his plate, he likely would have made the connection to the NYSP and determined next of kin through their notification database. I exited the slider and braced myself as I met the officers halfway.

"This can't be good," I said out of nervousness, emitting a half laugh, half cough. "I work in law enforcement, and I know they always send two officers when something bad happens." Foolish as it sounds now, this is the abnormal way I reacted to most everything during the following few hours.

The officers, sent from our town's police department, asked if we could go inside. I thought it strange that they couldn't give me bad news on the patio, but apparently there must be some protocol about it.

We went inside into the kitchen, where none of us sat down. There's been an accident, they said, a serious accident. Who is it, I demanded, tell me what's happened. Your parents were in a car accident, they said, in Pennsylvania. It was a serious accident. Take me to them, I demanded. I want to see them. Which hospital have they been taken to? You don't understand, the one officer said to me, then a pause. The second officer looked extremely uncomfortable. They were both eyeing me warily, like I might make a sudden, unexpected move at any moment.

Wait, I said, wait. Are you telling me that my parents are dead?? I had spoken with my mother less than 24 hours before. People are not simply here and then suddenly gone. It doesn't happen like that. It doesn't happen to people we know.

I'm sorry, the first officer said. Yes. And then … Is there anyone you can call? Any family nearby?

My husband is upstate getting his son at college, I said. I have a brother in New Jersey and a sister in Massachusetts. The officer asked if there was anyone local. He explained that they were not permitted to leave me alone, without a friend or family member to support me. I stepped away from the officers into the foyer and called my husband.

Like me, Eddie did not immediately grasp what I was telling him. There were things going on in the background on his end, and admittedly, I don't believe my voice was projecting very well. I had to say it a second time. "My parents were just killed in a car accident. The police are here. They can't leave me alone, apparently." Eddie didn't know what to say but clearly slipped into action after we ended our call. Within half an hour, his parents, sister, and nephew were at our house, standing in for my family that was suddenly much smaller than it had been that morning.

Now, I had to make the two hardest phone calls I will ever make in my lifetime. I cannot recall whom I called first, my brother Tom or my sister Terry. I think it was Tom, because he was geographically closer. Fortunately, I found him at home, and we spoke while his two daughters watched TV in the other room. There's nothing worse than someone answering the phone with a tone of pleasant surprise in his voice, and then me having to turn all serious right away. I asked if he was at home to which he responded in the affirmative. I told him that there had been an accident and that Mom and Dad were dead. He grasped it much faster than I did. I told him that I had to call Terry but would speak with him a little later.

It was even worse calling my sister, because she had just returned from a three-month sabbatical to Buenos Aires, Argentina, earlier that week. She had spoken to our mother more than once, but she and I had not yet talked. She answered the phone with a cheerful "*Hola!*" and asked if I was calling to welcome her back. She was looking forward to discussing her trip with me since I had also spent time in Latin America. I asked if we could speak seriously for a minute, then asked if she was at home. And then I told her as well.

## The Post-Mortem Marathon

When someone dies, there are so many details that have to be worked out immediately. There is no true grace period when a death occurs. You are immediately making crucial and costly decisions with no preamble or preparation. I don't know what guided me in those first few hours, but it was a gift of grace that led me through those steps when I still didn't fully, truly believe that my parents were gone. All I had was someone's word but no evidence—not yet.

My parents had been killed on an interstate in Pennsylvania, so the first matter of business was bringing their bodies back to New Jersey. I called my parent's parish, St. Peter the Apostle in Parsippany, New Jersey, and spoke with a lovely person in the office there. I still don't know why she was working on a Saturday afternoon, but again, the stars aligned to facilitate the process for me. After offering her sincere sympathy, the woman asked if she could help with anything.

I explained that, of course, the funeral would be at St. Peter's, but could she recommend a funeral home to take care of the arrangements? (I left out the part about retrieving the bodies.) She suggested the Stephen J. Priola Funeral Service in Lake Hiawatha (a section of Parsippany close to my parents' home), with whom many parishioners had had positive experiences.

Again, I lucked out, if I can be permitted to say such a thing on the day my parents died. Stephen was respectful, sympathetic, and efficient—exactly what you need when you don't know what the heck you are doing, and you are too emotionally wrecked to comprehend the situation.

He assured me that his home would retrieve the bodies from Pennsylvania, and then asked when we would like to come in to discuss arrangements for the wake and the funeral. Tomorrow, I answered—my sister had immediately made arrangements to travel down by train, and my brother had arranged childcare (his actress wife Liz McCartney was on tour with a Broadway show but flew home as soon as she could).

Our meeting with Stephen the following day was, frankly, as painless as it could possibly be. He walked us through the steps, promised to take care of all of the details, and gave us options as to what was and was not required for the mausoleum burial. We selected lovely caskets—a pale blue for our mother and a burgundy for our father ("merlot," I believe it was called, so we knew immediately that it was the right choice for our wine-loving father). And best of all, Stephen understood that it would take some time for us to get access to our parents' bank accounts and said that no payment was due right away. We could pay the (double) funeral bill once we had accessed the money. Another blessing!

Next, we had to go over to our parents' house. Eddie joined us. Not entirely sure where to begin, we followed logic. We went through the house and removed any valuables (there were not many, as our parents were not spend-y), grabbed checkbooks, and sought out any stashes of cash. My mother had gone to the ATM recently and had hidden a bank envelope with $270 in cash. We all agreed that it was very considerate of her to leave an amount easily divisible by three. Then, we checked windows and doors, reviewed the thermostat settings, confirmed the lights were on timers, and locked up the house.

The following day, Monday, someone had to drive out to Pennsylvania to pick up my parents' belongings. It turns out that the funeral home had our authority to retrieve the bodies from the medical examiner's office there, but they did not have the authority to retrieve possessions from the car. Thankfully, Eddie offered to drive Tom out to the garage where my parents' car—or what was left of it—had been taken.

Eddie courageously removed all necessary items from the vehicle (my mother's purse, my dad's wallet, the luggage they had each packed for my uncle's funeral, documents, and the brand-new trench coat that my mother had carefully laid across the backseat). Tom saw the state of the car (completely crushed over the front seat, which clearly no human could have survived) and could not bear to approach the vehicle.

While they were in Pennsylvania, Terry and I took care of other logistics, including the ever-important (in Irish-American culture) repast after the funeral. Because we had to allow time for all of the Moynahan relatives to make arrangements to travel from my uncle's funeral in Erie, Pennsylvania, to my parents' double funeral in Parsippany, New Jersey (I still feel tremendous guilt about putting all those poor people through this), the wake would not be held until

Wednesday afternoon and evening, with the funeral on Thursday morning. The repast was scheduled for lunchtime on Thursday, and for the location, we chose Don Pepe's Steakhouse in Pine Brook, New Jersey, a lovely place favored by my parents which served Spanish and Portuguese cuisine. We gave the restaurant an approximate headcount (way too low as it would turn out).

Terry and I went clothes shopping to find appropriately somber outfits for the wake and funeral. I miraculously found a stylish, but on sale, black dress, and Terry also had luck. We made appointments at a local hair salon for Wednesday morning so that we would at least have "good hair" for the wake and funeral. We were about to see people we hadn't seen in years, so we might as well look our best while we were at our worst.

## En Bref, A Good Funeral

Lucky. That is the only way to put it for how things went with the funeral arrangements, our agreement on what Mom and Dad would have wanted, the turnout for the two sessions of the wake, and the tremendous support we received at the funeral.

Although we did our best to contact as many people as we could (and to ask them to contact others), I was profoundly humbled at the number and diversity of people who came out for us at the wake. There were old college mates of my father's. Some women my mother had worked with at The Seeing Eye in Morristown, New Jersey. Relatives galore from both families came out. There was hearty representation from my office (a benefit of working in law enforcement, there is always a remarkable showing when a member suffers a loss) and from my brother's office, both in Manhattan.

There were people from high school that the three of us barely remembered. There were new friends who technically had never met our parents. And there were random community members who simply wanted to pay their respects. We noticed a shy man standing back from the crowd at the second session of the wake. It took us a moment or two, but then we realized that it was the Argentinean owner of our parents' favorite local restaurant! He had seen their photos in the obituary section of the newspaper and had made a point to offer his respects. Astounding and beautiful.

The funeral mass was well attended, and again, the presence of those who came humbled me. As my husband is with the NYSP, we had an excellent representation from his troop, many acting unofficially as both transport and security. I gave the eulogy, which I was able to write two days before without so much as an ounce of difficulty. The words just came, and with a few tweaks by my brother and sister, I was ready.

Granted, I had Eddie stand right behind me at the lectern just in case I had a breakdown while I was up there. I didn't, but it was still comforting to know he was there. In fact, he was my anchor throughout the whole ordeal, and his presence was made all the more remarkable considering that we had only been married for a year and a half. Not exactly the kind of thing you expect to go through as newlyweds!

Only close family and friends accompanied us to the mausoleum in East Hanover, New Jersey, where there was a brief service. We then proceeded to the Portuguese restaurant, which was already filled with funeral attendees who did not feel it was their place to go to the cemetery. The party was well underway with food and drink in ample supply.

It was the last party my parents would ever throw, so we didn't want to limit the festivities in any way, especially since so many people had traveled so far. I spoke with friends from college, Tom and Monique, who had driven up from Washington, DC at some ridiculous hour that morning to make the funeral. Monique told a funny story about one of her triplet daughters, a toothbrush, and her butt—completely irreverent but very welcome at the time. I couldn't believe I was laughing on the day of my parents' funeral, but considering that humor was a large part of how we related to each other in our family, it seemed appropriate.

I glanced over to a long table where my aunt, uncle, and my aunt's three sisters—all of whom had traveled down from Massachusetts for the funeral—were happily ensconced next to a group of NYSP investigators who had offered assistance that morning. As I looked on, one of the investigators poured himself a glass of sangria and exclaimed, "I feel like I'm in Portugal!" A successful event by any standard.

When everyone had left and it was just me, Eddie, and my brother and sister (the investigators had escorted other close family back to the cars they had left at the funeral home), we four agreed that it had been a luncheon befitting our parents. And then we got the bill.

Let's just say that a good time was had by all—and by all, I mean many, many more people than we had anticipated. But on this one occasion, the dollar figure didn't bother us—once the initial shock wore off.

# INTRODUCTION

## Death, The Great Equalizer

As has often been said, none of us gets out of this life alive. That's part of the deal: live your allocated portion of time on earth and then move on to the great beyond. The good news is that, rich or poor, we all go, and all that we acquire in this lifetime stays behind. The bad news is that someone has to gather up all that is left, catalog it, and distribute it according to the deceased's wishes. Unless the person died intestate (e.g., without a will) in which case the state determines how to distribute everything—not the preferred way to go.

Many people dread the task of serving as an executor—It's depressing! It's labor intensive! I am not compensated for my time and effort! Yes, yes, and yes. Except that I (now) believe that accepting this responsibility may be the very thing that allows you to grieve, honor, and learn about your loved one—an unexpected inheritance, you might say.

I like to say that the deceased are people, too. Every estate is different, just like the deceased person was! No two estates are alike, and no instruction manual could ever cover all of the possible situations you might encounter as you administer your loved one's estate. But there is some commonality among every estate, and there are bits of knowledge and experience that will benefit you if and when you are faced with the task.

And that is exactly why we are here. The whole point of this book is to help you accomplish three essentials tasks:

1.  Administer your loved one's estate.
2.  Preserve more of their assets.
3.  Draw closer to your loved one and protect their legacy through this process.

(You can tell that this is important because I increased the font size.)

In each of the subsequent chapters, you will encounter topics falling under one of the above themes. I suspect that you may have picked up this book because you are seeking further knowledge regarding Tasks 1 and 2. Fair enough. However, if Task 3 completely disinterests you, perhaps this isn't the book for you. My reason for starting my business—and for writing this book—is inextricably tied to my memories of, and respect for, my parents, Bart and Mary. Ain't no successful estate administration without the love, people!

## Some Ground Rules

I fully admit that I am not an estate attorney. But, as the saying goes, I have lived it. My impetus for writing this book was simple: If I (someone who is analytical by nature and experienced in investigations by trade) found serving as executrix to be a challenge, then how would someone with a young family, a demanding job, and/or zero time be able to do this? Think of me as the Common Man, tossed into this predicament and forced to fend for myself in the world of estate administration. I learned A LOT, and now it's time for me to share this knowledge with you.

Please note this important disclaimer: Nothing in this book is meant to serve as legal advice. In fact, I heartily recommend (in chapter 4) that you DO retain an estate attorney with whom you can consult on all of the points mentioned here (and many more that would not fit in this tiny tome). With that being said, let's not break the bank, shall we?

You'll notice that I flit between using the terms executor, personal representative, and trustee. (I also use the term estate attorney when some of these practitioners go by the titles estate planner and/or probate attorney.) Your estate attorney will let you know what his/her title is and what your title is, just as he/she will let you know whether you are dealing with an estate, a trust, or some other estate planning vehicle in regard to your deceased loved one. The process is largely the same: you still must *find* the assets before they can be distributed.

I will default to using the terms *executor* and *estate*, for simplicity's sake. That was my direct experience, and it is currently the most common circumstance.

I wish I could be there to walk you through this process … to go through the boxes and the photo albums … to open the new mail and to sort through the old, yellowed documents … to help you make those phone calls to the umpteenth financial institution or to write letters (sometimes more than once) to request account closures … and to try to determine what the heck is in the Tupperware in the back of your loved one's fridge. For some of you, I can be there. (Please see the end of this book or my website for ways you can work with me.) But for the majority of you, dear readers, allow me to be your Yoda, magically appearing when you need me and offering sage, grammatically creative lessons to guide you through what will arguably be one of the most trying times in your life.

Remember: The Force transcends life and death, and so do your feelings for your loved one.

# Chapter One

# THE RECKONING

## Somewhere in Northern New Jersey ...

Scene: The conference room at the offices of my parents' estate attorney, Christopher Rohde

Date: One day after my parents' funeral

Those present: Chris, another attorney with the firm, myself, my brother Tom, and my sister Terry

Purpose: To meet with the estate attorney, have him explain the terms of my parents' wills, and discuss next steps

Mood: Still in shock and grieving, just beginning to process everything that had happened over the prior six days

The first thing we learn is that the three of us are very lucky. Not just because we had wonderful parents who prepared for this day years in advance, not just because we ended up with an estate attorney who is both knowledgeable and compassionate, and not just because our parents' frugality throughout their lives—embarrassing as it occasionally was while we were growing up—meant that a number of our financial concerns were about to be allayed.

We're lucky because, as with most of our experiences from birth to the present, our parents gave us more than they reserved for themselves. This generosity of spirit was something we acknowledged but never fully absorbed, until now.

Years before, our parents had gone full throttle on their estate planning. (I should say here that my mother went full throttle. My father went kicking and screaming, fully resisting the idea of planning—and paying—for anything having to do with death. But once on board, he made sure that they did it right.) I suppose that after burying their own parents and several siblings, not to mention attending numerous friends' funerals over the years, they were aware of just how difficult—or how streamlined—one could make one's death and its aftermath.

Utilizing an excellent estate planning law firm, they had rewritten their wills, established a life-insurance trust, put into place living wills and end-of-life wishes, purchased joint mausoleum "deeds," and paid for it all upfront. (Well, almost all … more on that later.) Chris quickly reassured us that everything was in place and that our parents, in fact, had made this moment much easier than we had likely anticipated.

We already knew the terms of the wills—"Split evenly three ways!" as my mother had often proclaimed—but didn't yet know the full benefit of their planning. We also knew that I was to be executrix. While I spent six years overseas serving at U.S. embassies, my brother had been the named executor. But as I soon as I returned to A-mer-i-ca, my parents had switched the estate duties over to me, with my brother's full blessing. I was analytical, organized, detail-oriented, and a nerd extraordinaire— exactly the type of person you want to administer your estate. I loved lists. I loved marking things off lists. I was in my element, even if I was a weeping mess.

There were no real surprises—nothing at all like the reading of a will on a television drama. No secret love children, no secret millions, no secrets—period. Our parents divided their estates as they lived, with everything above board, spelled out, and prepared. It was the soft landing that our parents had planned (I refer to their wills, obviously, not their deaths), and with Chris as their estate attorney, we had direction and a rudder by which to steer.

After providing an overview of everything that needed to be done— made even more complex due to the fact that we were dealing with simultaneous deaths—Chris turned to me and said the words that would have a greater impact than either of us realized at the time. "You know, you can save a lot of money in legal fees by doing much of the estate work yourself. Of course, we will accompany you throughout this process, but many of the tasks are ones that you can assume on your own."

I felt, rather than saw, my brother's and sister's heads turn in my direction.

"Yes," I said. "Yes, of course. I will take care of as much of it as I can."

And here, my friends, is where we begin …

## Chapter Two

# SECURE THE RANCH

In the world of events that involve numerous details, a death in the family is second only to a wedding. And there is no cake (although there may be sangria). With that being said, do it right, and you will have a much easier time of it. Identifying and preserving your loved one's assets is a priority, and for most people, their largest asset is their home.

In this chapter, I focus on what to do in the immediate aftermath of your loved one's passing—say, in the first week after the loss. We'll discuss more comprehensive steps to identifying assets in later chapters. This is a quick, hit-the-basics kind of checklist.

## Reminder Regarding Priorities

Before proceeding to the list of first steps below, I would like to clarify something. In the days following your loved one's death, your first responsibility is to the deceased and his/her family. The estate and its assets are secondary to the people. You will want to allow time to process the loss before making any major moves with the estate anyway. When you do begin, approach estate administration as a tribute to the deceased. If you view it as an opportunity to do one last thing for that person, it makes it an honor rather than a burden.

And you will need that positive mindset for the work ahead.

# Initial Steps Following A Loss

Assuming your loved one lived alone, and their residence will now be empty, you need to secure it to the degree possible. There are a tiny number of individuals on the planet who will take advantage of a recent death and target the empty home—sometimes, unbelievably, while the funeral is occurring, the date and time of which is helpfully listed in your loved one's obituary. It is unlikely that one of these miscreants, who will surely occupy a special level of Dante's Hell someday, will target your loved one. But better safe than sorry.

So take reasonable measures to secure the home. If keys were held by a number of different people, including neighbors and acquaintances, you may wish to change the locks. Use the alarm system, if there is one, and put several lights on timers so that the home appears lived in. Enlist the assistance of trusted neighbors: this is one of those occasions in which the nosy, stay-at-home neighbor is a gift. Let them know about the death (they likely already do) and ask for their help "keeping an eye on the place." Make sure all of the windows and doors are locked. Walk around the entire home, outside and in, to check for problem areas, leaks, and points of entry.

Unplug unnecessary electronics, and ensure that smoke and carbon-monoxide detectors are in working order. Remove any firearms or other weapons. Take valuables (watches, fine jewelry, cash, credit cards, and checkbooks) to your home for safekeeping.

If essential documents are easy to collect (e.g., they are already stored in a box or file cabinet), move them to your home. Set the thermostat to a reasonable temperature (at minimum to prevent the pipes from freezing).

Your priority while going through your loved one's home in the first few days following their death is to secure the premises, but it is very closely followed by locating important documents related to your loved one and his/her funeral plans and estate. So in your initial search of the home, keep an eye out for the following documents: the will or trust; funeral or burial instructions; prearranged funeral documents, including the deed to a cemetery or mausoleum plot and other prepaid funeral arrangements; birth, marriage, death, and adoption certificates; military separation papers; Social Security cards; property and tax documents; safe-deposit keys or proof of a box at the bank; and deeds to the home and cars.

Do not be alarmed if you don't immediately find all of these documents on the first pass. Obviously, funeral documents are the real time-sensitive ones. But as long as you're doing a quick pass through the home, you might as well kill a few birds with one stone.

Complete a change-of-address with the U.S. Postal Service to start receiving your loved one's mail at your own home. Nowadays, you can do it online, so it really is a quick and easy way to make sure that no mail goes to the empty residence (and therefore no one can steal mail from the mailbox).

☼ **As soon as practical, forward your loved one's mail to your own address. Mail is a primary source of financial information and will continue to be so throughout the estate administration process.**

Consider canceling cable, phone, and Internet service if you don't need it at the house. Caveat here: I myself was reluctant to cancel our parents' phone service at the house (and on my mother's cell phone) because I didn't want to lose the voicemail messages with my mother's voice. Terry and I called the numbers more than once between their deaths and the funeral, just to hear it. (Our father did not enjoy talking on the phone, so his voice was not recorded.) You may wish to memorialize the message in some way, so that you can replay it repeatedly while grieving and eating ice cream. Just a thought.

Cancel newspaper delivery immediately (a collection of papers at the end of the driveway is a clear sign to burglars that no one is living there). Decide whether you will maintain the lawn, driveway, and sidewalk yourself or whether you should change the lawn, leaf, and snow accounts to your name.

Do NOT cancel the utilities at the home. By this, I am referring to electricity, gas, and water. It may seem like a quick way to save a few bucks each month while administering the estate, but it is not the way to go. Resist the temptation. For one thing, it is very difficult to show a home for sale without lights, heat, and plumbing. If you are still tempted, allow me to briefly provide a cautionary tale.

My uncle Danny, who suffered a debilitating stroke and was eventually confined to a long-term care facility, had a small home out of state. My mother held my uncle's power of attorney, so it was up to her to liquidate my uncle's assets, exhaust the money from the sale of those items to pay for his care, and then sign him up to have his care covered by Medicaid. My mother did a very good job of all this, attempting to preserve as much as possible to go towards his care. She decided to turn off the utilities at the empty home, since the weather was good and there was no concern about freezing pipes. She drove out to the home periodically to remove items, sell his vehicles and tools, and take care of other details. She never stayed more than a couple of hours.

Then in August, she and I were scheduled to spend five days (staying in a local motel) to deal with the more detail-oriented aspects of emptying his home in order to prepare it for sale. I flew in from where I was working out of the country, and we drove the 90 minutes or so to the house to begin our work. It soon became apparent that shutting off the utilities was not one of her brightest moves. For one, we could only work there while the sun was out, because cleaning out a home by flashlight is neither effective nor efficient.

We also found it necessary to drive into town a few times a day to find an establishment in which to use the facilities. After an unfortunate lunch choice by my mother one day, we returned to the house for the afternoon to continue working. Within an hour, my mother was patently unwell, and—lacking a working toilet—we had to MacGyver a solution to allow her to … get rid of her unwellness. Since I promised myself that this book would not contain scatological humor, I will have to leave the rest to your imagination.

## Notifications

While at your loved one's home, keep an eye out for an address book or other list of contacts. You will need this information in order to make notifications to distant family and friends, as well as former work colleagues of your loved one. If you can access your loved one's cell phone, you should document or download their contact list. The same is true if you can access your loved one's computer, specifically their email accounts. All of these are excellent places to find the contact information for those your loved one would want to know of their passing. Review the names on incoming emails as well as those in the Saved and Trash folders. Sure, fifty percent of it will be spam, but at least some of the communications will have merit!

Although not a priority in the days immediately following your loved one's death, it will be necessary, at some point, to notify the deceased's doctors, membership organizations, and holiday card acquaintances. Again, don't look to do this during days one through seven following the passing, but it should be done when things calm down a bit.

## Things to Consider:

- ☐ *Focus on people first, then the estate and its assets.*
- ☐ *Secure the home to the degree possible.*
- ☐ *Search for and collect important documents—especially those related to the funeral and burial.*
- ☐ *Have your loved one's mail forwarded to your address.*
- ☐ *Cancel newspapers but not utilities.*
- ☐ *Look for an address book or download a phone or email contact list to facilitate making notifications.*

## Chapter Three

# "It'll Make a Nice Sandwich"

**Waste Not, Want Not**

One of the great constants in our lives as Moynahans is that food is a priority, a gift, a blessing, and a burden. I have met families that do not eat leftovers; ones that go out to eat three times a week and order in for the other meals; ones that keep very little food in the house in the first place. Ours was never one of those families.

I've talked about how we secured our parents' home the day after their deaths. We also followed an ingrained commandment that stated we should consume or share all edible food within the confines of the house. Our father was born during the Depression and never met a food scrap that he wouldn't eat. Our mother grew up in a poor household with five people in a two-bedroom, New York City apartment (but as she explained, everyone else's family was in the same boat, so they didn't know they were poor!).

We learned from a young age not to waste food and never to take it for granted. My father's favorite expression, when we attempted to throw out an undesirable piece of food, condiment, or scrap, was, "Don't throw that out—it'll make a nice sandwich!" This was in no way true, but it did become a resounding chorus marking our growing-up years (and ever after).

Since our parents had not anticipated dying that day, their fridge, freezer, and pantry had a good amount of food in them. We divvied up the perishable food first: my sister didn't live in the area so obviously couldn't take any of it, and my brother really only took the food items that our parents had specifically bought for his young daughters when our parents were babysitting them at their house. So that left a pile of food for me and Eddie to transport from Parsippany to our own home.

Here is what we did and what we learned:

Remove perishable food within the first week! I know that there are many pressing issues following a death, but decaying food in an empty home does not lighten the load. Eat what you can of fresh food. Canned goods, nonperishable food, baking ingredients, and spices can be distributed (or donated) later. If something is past its marked expiration date, do not donate it to a local food bank. You can eat it yourself if you feel it's still good, but do not clog up charitable coffers with food that they can't distribute.

One word regarding spices: I found spice containers with Pathmark stickers on them. I happen to know that our parents stopped shopping at Pathmark sometime in the 1990s. This was a clear indicator to me to throw out those spices. Newer spices (purchased within this millennium) went home with me, but some were eventually tossed as well since they had lost their flavor.

Also important: empty all garbage cans and wastebaskets in and around the home. You don't want them to attract bugs or rodents, and you don't want to mutter "What's that smell??" every time you visit the home. If you are not sure of the days for garbage pickup and recycling in your loved one's neighborhood, now is the time to learn. You will have many opportunities to put out garbage and recyclables over the next few months.

Not a first-seven-days task: Cleaning out the pantry and cabinets—thou shall waste nothing! Eddie and I took home all of the plastic wrap, aluminum foil, sandwich bags, trash bags, and parchment paper. There were multiples of each because it appeared that, after a certain age, my parents didn't bother to look in the back of drawers and cabinets any longer and simply purchased a new box of whatever item they couldn't reach. We used their supplies for years following their deaths, just as my parents had used my uncle's supplies for years after his death. It's a family tradition. It made me sad when we finally used the last sandwich bag—it was as if another link to my parents was now gone. But I know for a fact that they were smiling in heaven as they saw us "use up" these items.

# The Frugality Mentality

## "That's how we put you through college."

At our parents' 50th anniversary dinner (celebrated just six months prior to their passing), Terry asked Mom and Dad how they had done it all on one salary. After all, they had three children, a four-bedroom house in a nice neighborhood in a high-tax state, and three (private) college educations that they largely paid for. They handled it all on my father's modest salary until my mother began working again after the first two of us went off to college.

I recall my father humbly shrugging off the compliment as my mother agreed that it had been difficult but worth it. They looked pleased that we (finally) acknowledged their many sacrifices and marveled at their resourcefulness, especially because we were now facing similar financial challenges in our own lives.

We weren't always so understanding of the financial constraints placed upon us. My father especially embraced the frugal lifestyle—mind you, he wasn't a minimalist; he just didn't like to spend money—and had difficulty relaxing a bit once the pressure was off. My mother was intrinsic to the financial survival of our family growing up, but she was more comfortable spending a little after we were successfully launched into adulthood.

In addition to never wasting an ounce of food, my father would wear his underwear until it literally fell off him, all stretched-out waistband and holes in the butt. He owned the same faded pair of jeans through five presidential administrations. He kept the soaps and shampoos from hotel visits for years, collecting them in a basket "for guests." When questioned as to these extreme practices, my father would reply, "But that's how we're putting you through college." Later, this took on the past tense and became "That's how we put you through college."

I must admit, it is true that the careful way our parents handled money throughout their lives did allow us to take out smaller student loans than we otherwise would have had to. My parents covered what they could of each semester's tuition, took advantage of financial aid to include grants and work study, and then signed Stafford loans for us for the difference. In high school, my father had pleaded with me to attend an in-state (New Jersey) college or university since I had been offered 50% tuition at many of them. (This was during a period in which New Jersey's high-achieving students famously left the state to attend college.) He even promised to buy me a used car if I stayed in-state.

However, being eighteen and self-involved, I shrugged off the financial burden I was about to place on my parents' shoulders and insisted on going to my high-priced university of choice. My mother, despite being very intelligent, had been denied the chance to go to college by her father and their financial circumstances. She supported my decision and told my father, "Let her go to the best college she can get into!"

So I did—two years after my brother had entered another private university and five years before my sister Terry started at her private university. I vaguely understood that my parents had had to take out a second mortgage in order to finance our higher educations, but I never asked many questions or apologized. I did pay off my undergrad student loans in less than the allotted ten years, so at least I did not shift *that* financial burden to my parents.

But when it came time for graduate school after I had been in the workforce for a few years, I knew that I was on my own. My parents had made it clear that they would do what they could for four years of our undergraduate educations, but they did not have the resources for graduate school. So I worked 32 hours per week to pay for my food, housing, and incidentals, and I financed 100% of the tuition for the two years it took me to get my master's degree. I had a substantial loan balance at the end of it, along with a shiny degree and a new appreciation for my parents and their generosity.

I have learned a few things about this subject since my parents' deaths. For one, as I went through the mortgage and other financial documents kept in my parents' safe-deposit box, I discovered that they hadn't taken out a second mortgage but rather a homeowner's line of credit to help finance our expensive universities. And, they took it out in 1983 … meaning it wasn't initially for my college tuition but for my brother's. I know that they tapped it for my education two years later, but I wasn't the impetus.

Guilt is so much better when it's shared.

I also now understand Dad's famous grimace of financial pain when it came time for my stepchildren to attend college. I recall thinking, "Why go to the $60,000-a-year private university when you can receive an excellent education from the $40,000-a-year private university, or better yet, the $20,000-a-year state university??" I knew the extensive sacrifices my husband and I would have to make for the seven years that his kids would overlap in college (they, too, were instructed and adhered to the four-year plan), and my fear almost got the better of me.

But then, from the back of my mind, I heard my mother's voice saying, "Bart, let her go to the college of her choice!" And so, we did. And, like my parents, we survived paying a large portion of it and limiting the amount of student loans the kids had to take out.

## The Proposal

Interestingly, my father's frugality DID allow him to plan for my eventual, long-delayed, can't-believe-it-finally-happened wedding in 2010. You would think as the decades passed without being called upon to pay for a wedding that my father would have reallocated that fund for other purposes. But he did not (I don't think my mother would have let him anyway). And he was as excited as anyone when the day finally came ... as exhibited by the victorious fist he raised when he and my mother were announced at our wedding reception. (I asked him later why he did that, and he shrugged and said, "It felt right.")

I would love to have been a fly on the wall for the occasion when my husband asked my parents for my hand in marriage. I obviously was not present, but my husband recounted the scene to me in such vivid imagery that I really feel like I was there.

Eddie and I had discussed marriage, but he had not proposed nor even picked up the ring when he decided it was time to "do the right thing" and ask my parents. Granted, I was 42 years old at this point and had been out of the house since I came home for summers between college. I had moved multiple times, lived overseas in three countries, and was admittedly pretty long in the tooth. But my husband, ever the gentleman, thought it would show respect to continue the quaint practice of asking for my hand. Knowing that my mother had an equal—if not stronger—say in such things, he intended to ask them both.

Eddie called my parents early in the work week and got my father on the phone. My father, not a big phone talker, for once did not immediately pass the phone to my mother. Since he was hard of hearing for, oh, the last 20 years of his life, Eddie had to tell him twice who was calling.

"Mr. Moynahan, this is Eddie Diaz."

"I'm sorry. Who is this??"

"It's Eddie. Eileen's boyfriend."

(Awkward pause)

"Oh, Eddie! Hi, Eddie—how are you?"

"Good, Mr. Moynahan. I am calling to see if I could come over sometime this week after work and speak with you and your wife."

(My father calls out to my mother) "Mary, it's Eddie. He wants to know if he can come over and speak with us this week."

(My mother speaking in the background, responding with an overly enthusiastic, "Yes, yes, of course! Tell him we're free any day this week.")

"Hello, Eddie? Mary says we'd love to speak with you. When would you like to come over?"

"Well, I was thinking of coming over Thursday evening after work. How about 7:00 p.m.?"

(My father, again, speaking to my mother) "Mary, Eddie wants to come over Thursday around 7:00 p.m."

(My mother answering him, with her voice an octave higher than before, "Yes, yes!!! Thursday at 7:00 is good!!!! We'll be here!!!!!")

"Ha ha … yes, Eddie. We'll see you Thursday! Thank you! Thanks for calling!"

Eddie pretty much knew that they were going to say yes. But if there had been any question, the number of exclamation points likely reassured him.

A few days passed, and Eddie made the long schlep out from Manhattan to Parsippany on the always-congested route to the suburbs. He cannot recall whether he pulled into the driveway or parked along the curb in front of the house. He DOES, however, clearly recall the visual that greeted him as he walked up the sidewalk. My parents were standing next to each other with the wooden door open wide and the screen door in front of them.

They were jostling for position to fit into the screen's opening, each with huge, stupid grins on their faces. He doesn't know how long they were standing there, but they had clearly been watching out the window to know when he arrived. Not wanting to give Eddie the chance to drive away should he change his mind, they were ready to throw open the screen door and give chase.

Fortunately for everyone involved, Eddie did not change his mind and walked to the front door ... which was opened for him before he had even reached the steps.

"Come in, Eddie! Come in!!" they cried enthusiastically, almost in unison.

The screen door shut. The front door was closed after him. There might have been the click of a lock—Eddie is fuzzy on that part. He was promptly ushered to the kitchen. My parents did not immediately sit.

"Please, Eddie—have a seat!" Huge grins continued to face him. Eddie sat down in the proffered chair at the kitchen table. My mother sat to Eddie's right, in her usual seat. My father sat across from her, to Eddie's left. Grin. Grin.

Now, let me reiterate here, my husband is a senior investigator with the New York State Police. At the time this was all going down, he had 25 years in law enforcement under his belt. He had studied martial arts as a younger man. He had taught defensive tactics at the State Police Academy in Albany. He had read Sun Tzu's *The Art of War*. He had studied military history and watched countless programs about battle strategy on The History Channel. How he did not realize that he was being flanked is beyond me! The poor kid didn't stand a chance. He was trapped, and he had no supporting army. No general was coming to save him. No aerial support was available.

As all generals know, when you have no way to retreat, you must simply push forward.

"Uh, yes, Mr. and Mrs. Moynahan, as you know... [blah blah blah blah, blah blah blah...]"

(This portion is being edited for content. It doesn't really matter what my husband said. He could have discussed the weather. Asked about their health. Talked about the Yankees. Spoken in Swahili. It. Does. Not. Matter. What Bart and Mary Moynahan heard on that warm, late-September day was, "Eddie wants to marry your daughter. This is the opportunity you have been waiting 20 years for! Do not let this man escape. Do not let this man pass go.")

But what they said was, "Why yes! That would be wonderful, Eddie!! We would be very happy for you to join our family!!!" More huge grins. A round of hugs and handshakes. Some watery eyes of joy. And then, from Mary, in a falsely-casual, high-pitched voice...

"Bart, can you go to the fridge and get us something to celebrate?"

Out of the fridge came a bottle of champagne. Faster than you could say "Bonsai!", three glasses were produced. Note: Eddie had walked in with a paper bag in his hand, which contained a split of champagne. But Mary and Bart were already prepared for this possibility. I'm guessing that my mother sent my father out to purchase this bottle right after they got off the phone with Eddie a few days before. As celebrations go, this was one highly anticipated bottle of bubbly!

Eddie cannot recall whether they drank both my parents' bottle and his bottle of champagne. My parents had eaten dinner two hours before so didn't offer Eddie anything to eat. They all enjoyed a glass or two of champagne. Eventually, Eddie got up to go, and my parents escorted him to the door. They all said goodbye, and Eddie walked to his car. As he turned the car on and prepared to drive home, he turned one last time toward the front door of my parents' house. There they stood, jostling for position in the frame of the screen door, huge grins on their faces, waving goodbye a little *too* enthusiastically.

Eddie had just given my parents one of the happiest moments of their lives. And to his endless credit, my soon-to-be fiancé did not run away in terror.

## Dueling Wedding Budgets

This brings to mind the discussion I had with Mom and Dad about the budget for my upcoming wedding. I was worried, in advance, about their differing opinions as to the wedding budget, which turned out to be unnecessary and, in fact, rather amusing!

The three of us sat down at the kitchen table—where all important discussions happened in our family—to discuss the topic. I planned to pay for as much of the wedding as I could myself, but I knew that wouldn't get us beyond a nice lunch. So I decided to ask my parents outright what they would be comfortable contributing to the wedding budget.

I knew something was up by my mother's expression; she appeared amused by something and anxious to get the "meeting" started. My father, on the other hand, had that vaguely nauseated look he got when he was about to be hit up for money. (I remembered it well from our college discussions.) My mother suggested that they each write down on a scrap of paper what figure they had in mind as their contribution. She got paper and pens for herself and my father and then proceeded to write something down. My father was anxiously looking over to try to see what she was writing. I felt bad for him in a way, but I was also curious as to what the outcome might be.

My father finally put pen to paper and wrote down a figure. It was time to reveal what was written on the dueling, wedding budget slips of paper! My father nervously slid his paper over to me, facedown, and my mother said, "Read it out loud!" I read the amount aloud and thanked my father for his generosity. Then he and I both turned to my mother for her reveal. My father licked his lips and shifted nervously in his seat. My mother had a secret smile on her face and slid her paper over to me, also facedown. I turned it over and read aloud, "Five thousand dollars more than whatever your father wrote."

We all laughed, my mother looking very pleased with herself and my father still looking pained but somewhat relieved. We had a deal.

## Things to Consider:

☐ *Remove perishable food items from the home and empty all garbage cans within the first week.*

☐ *Remove nonperishable food and kitchen items within a month. Check expiration dates on everything. Consider donating items that you cannot use (if unopened) to a food pantry or other charity.*

☐ *Take the time to recall and appreciate your loved one's values ... especially the zany ones!*

## Chapter Four

# IGNORE SHAKESPEARE: HIRE AN ESTATE ATTORNEY!

## Almost Everyone Needs an Attorney

I can't tell you how many times I have heard someone say—including potential clients—something akin to, "I don't need an attorney: Mom didn't own anything!" when I suggest that they consider hiring an estate attorney and/or an estate organizer to help them administer their loved one's estate. Most of their deceased loved ones owned their own homes, supported themselves without debt for many years in retirement, and had a full and interesting life. Yet their children assert that they "had nothing."

Almost every one of them is wrong.

It is truly rare that I come across an estate in which there is absolutely nothing to collect. If that were the case, there wouldn't be an estimated $58 billion held in state "unclaimed" accounts at any given time! And even on the small chance that your loved one didn't own much, can you guarantee that you know what paperwork to file and when? Because your estate attorney does.

If nothing else, enjoy a free consultation with an estate attorney in your area, preferably one who has been referred by someone you know and trust. Many attorneys will meet with you at no cost for 30 minutes to briefly discuss your case, and through that meeting, you will have a good idea what steps are legally required to close your loved one's estate.

Needless to say, if your loved one had their own estate attorney— one who drew up their will and other end-of-life paperwork and who actually met with your loved one regarding these matters—that is likely the correct attorney for you to use.

Ensure that the estate attorney you hire is knowledgeable about the laws in the specific state where your loved one lived. Although we would have loved to have utilized my parents' estate attorney, Chris Rohde, when my husband and I drew up our own wills and documents, he is a member of the New Jersey Bar Association and therefore recommended that we work with an attorney from our current state of residence, New York. Estate laws do vary from state to state, and you want to work with someone who is already familiar with the local requirements and court procedures, not one who says, "Let me research that and get back to you."

☼ **Much has been written about the difference between having a will and having a trust. Make sure that you know which one you are dealing with! It will affect everything from the claim forms you request to the tax documents you are required to complete.**

A good estate attorney can facilitate the entire process and prevent you from making costly (and/or illegal) mistakes. He/she can also help you set up the appropriate estate or trust bank account into which all assets should be deposited and out of which all debts should be paid. No commingling of monies!

The estate attorney will go over the terms of your loved one's will or trust, usually in the presence of the main beneficiaries to the estate. A recommendation here: everyone present should be a <u>named</u> beneficiary, not the spouse of a beneficiary, a child of a beneficiary, or God forbid the boyfriend or girlfriend of a beneficiary. Your loved one named you, not your entourage, and unless named, they are not entitled to a say or an opinion.

From this point on, you as the executor will be in regular contact with the estate attorney, which reduces confusion (as well as costs). However, it is your job (and an excellent idea overall) to keep all of the beneficiaries in the loop. The more you communicate with them, the better. If you keep them informed as to what's going on and engage them in group decisions, you will reduce the chance of strife. Do not distribute any estate money to the beneficiaries until the estate attorney tells you it is appropriate to do so, usually once the estate is drawing to a close but occasionally midway through when there are enough collected assets to meet the financial amounts specified.

As for the "stuff" left behind by your loved one, feel free to divide low-value clothes, belongings, and mementos fairly among beneficiaries. Any possibly high-value items (artwork, jewelry, collectibles) should first be appraised. Again, you want to follow the letter and spirit of your loved one's will, but you also want to make the process as relaxed and transparent as a death can be. In my observation, when one beneficiary feels disconnected or cut off from what is happening, he/she may begin to think they are "losing out" on something. By keeping everyone equally informed, there are no surprises and less discord.

You will have to file a regular tax return for the deceased before the next April 15th and then subsequent estate tax returns for each year the estate is open. Remember that some assets will pass outside of probate (such as life insurance, which goes directly to the beneficiaries), while most assets will be deposited into the estate account. You can use the estate account to pay estate-related expenses, such as for utilities and taxes on the home as well as the estate attorney, estate organizer, and other service providers. Do not mix personal and estate monies, and maintain a check register detailing every credit and debit in the estate account.

> ☼ **Keep a detailed check register for every asset deposited into the estate account and every payment made out of the estate account. Assuming your handwriting is legible, this listing can simply be copied come tax time. It will make life easier for you, your estate attorney, and the poor schmuck who has to prepare the personal, estate, and/or trust tax returns.**

A quick note about trusts: it has become far more common nowadays for upper-middle-class earners to put the majority of their assets in a trust in order to avoid the trouble (and exposure) of formal probate. Each asset must be individually titled in the name of the trust—to include real property, accounts, vehicles, investments, etc.—to pass through that trust upon the death of the trustee. (The person who takes over following the death of the owner/trustee is called the successor trustee. That would be you.)

But it is not unusual to find smaller assets that were never titled in the name of the trust or which are unanticipated, such as utility refunds or overpayments. Be sure to share with your attorney *everything* you locate, whether or not it is titled in the trust.

## Proof-of-Authority Documents

One of the things that I didn't know estate attorneys could facilitate was obtaining proof-of-authority for an executor to act on behalf of the deceased. You might think, as I did, that being named executor in your loved one's will would be sufficient to declare you as the rightful person to be handling their affairs. Like me, you'd be wrong! As the representative of a financial company from which my client was attempting to obtain information explained to me in perfectly concise terms, "Yes, your client was named as the successor trustee, but a will or trust is not a court document in and of itself." Ahhhhh. Deep man, really deep.

When you begin the claim process for your loved one's assets, each company or financial institution will ask you for a document showing your proof-of-authority to act as the personal representative for the estate or trust. Depending on your state, this proof may take different forms. But basically, it is a short document officially stating that the court declares you as the responsible party. Most asset holders will ask you for this document as well as the death certificate for the deceased before they will even *talk* to you about the accounts. Until you establish your authority, you are essentially a nonentity to them—a poseur, a wannabe.

As mentioned, this proof can take multiple forms, such as certification of your authority to act as successor trustee to your loved one's trust; a document from the surrogate court naming you as executor; or another such court document that marks you as the authorized party. It can be confusing to a civilian, but an estate attorney can help with all of these.

In our situation, I was required to obtain letters testamentary from the Surrogate Court of Morris County, the county in which my parents were residents at the time of their deaths. Left to my own devices, I would have had no idea how to proceed on that front. Our estate attorney, however, knew exactly what to do and how to do it efficiently. He sent over the appropriate documents to the surrogate court in advance so that when I showed up at my appointment, I was greeted very respectfully by a wonderful woman who served as the surrogate for the county.

All of the papers were already prepared, merely awaiting my signature. Within that half-hour visit, I had everything I needed to move forward with both estates, ensuring that I would be able to establish myself with any vendor, utility, or financial institution with whom I had to work to administer the estates.

This is merely one of the myriad ways in which our estate attorney made our lives—and subsequently, our grief—easier. Chris smoothed out the rough edges while speeding up a difficult process. And that, my friends, is money well spent. (Especially when the money's not yours to begin with!)

## Things to Consider:

- [ ] *Consult with an estate attorney, even if you don't believe that your loved one's estate merits it.*
- [ ] *As the executor, ensure that you are in regular communication with the estate attorney and with each beneficiary.*
- [ ] *Do not distribute any estate assets without first consulting with your attorney.*
- [ ] *Obtain the appropriate proof-of-authority documents as soon as possible in order to act on behalf of the estate.*

**Chapter Five**

# Separate the Wheat from the Chaff – The First Sort

## All Paper is Not Created Equal

When I speak with people about estates, I hear a common refrain: "Sure, dealing with all of their possessions is tough, but it's the PAPER that is overwhelming!" This is immediately followed by me asking, "Did we have the same father??!" Because Bart never met a piece of paper that he didn't retain for decades.

Think of yourself as a gold miner as you go through your loved one's home. Some items are easily distinguishable as recycling (newspapers, magazines, mass mailings, take-out menus), while other items are clearly sentimental (letters, cards, photos). Unsure? Keep it for now and make a decision on the second pass.

Remember, on the first pass, we're looking for financial and property leads. Any clue that might suggest an account, policy, stash, or anything else of value belonging to your deceased loved one is worth following. There's gold in them there piles! You are mining the house for clues to assets.

As you do a quick, first sort to identify financial documents, throw them into a bin or box. Don't worry about duplicates, or how many accounts you've found. This is the first sifting, and it's meant to go quickly and efficiently. Do not, under any circumstances, throw out any of these financial documents at this time, no matter how old.

Since so much is done online nowadays, you must also make an effort to locate passwords used by your loved one to access their computer, websites, and apps. Check especially carefully in the area around your loved one's computer, in their file drawers, under their desk blotter, or scribbled on a slip of paper in their wallet. Don't berate yourself if you are ultimately unable to "break into" the computer or smart phone; I too could not access everything that I would have liked to review on my mother's computer, and the world did not end. (As a stop-gap measure, I check online unclaimed databases every year, just to make absolutely sure that Bart and Mary don't have a wild asset left out there.)

Let me say this again—do not throw out ANY financial documents at this time, no matter how old. You can do a second review when you take the box to your home to go over. Additionally, keep all deeds, payoff notices, and end-of-year tax statements.

In general, paper is going to be the medium through which you best learn about your loved one and their assets. Despite the trend toward paperless living, we all need to preserve specific items in hard copy. Review it all, everything, at least once, so that you can feel confident that you are being thorough (and nosy).

On the occasions when I give my highly anticipated speaking engagements—say, for free at the local public library—I like to play a game with the attendees called "Lead or No Lead?" (That is pronounced with the long 'e', as in 'feed', not the short 'e', as in 'bed'. Completely changes the meaning if you misinterpret this point. Becomes more of a Quentin Tarantino film.)

In the game, I describe a document, theoretically taken from the home of a deceased loved one, and ask the audience whether the document serves as a lead (or not) to possible assets held by the estate. Some of the documents are easily identifiable as leads (a bank statement listing an annual fee for the rental of a safe-deposit box), while some are less obvious (a pension statement dated 1974 for a company you never knew your loved one worked for).

The purpose of this exercise is to get you to think like an investigator and to at least allow for the possibility that this document could indicate assets. With an estate, there are many occasions for "pleasant surprises," so don't be too quick to dismiss something that doesn't immediately scream "money."

One of my proudest, you-da-bomb estate moments was when I was doing a second pass through documents taken from my parents' home. I had already identified, claimed, and received payment for the vast majority of their assets (the low-hanging fruit, so to speak) when I came across a generic letter from Hartford Life, asking whether my mother would like to purchase additional death and dismemberment (D&D) insurance above the free coverage she had as a customer.

Further investigation revealed that this company offered a basic amount of insurance to its long-term clients as a perk, in the hopes that they would purchase additional insurance at competitive rates. Sure, the basic benefit was a mere $1,000 ($500 if your loved one was over 70 years old, as my mother was), but this is free money. For the cost of a phone call (free) followed by a claim letter (50 cents) with a copy of the death certificate, I received a check for $500 to add to the estate.

I recognize that many people wouldn't bother to claim this small amount, but hey, that helped cover the cost of repairs to my parents' front walk, which is one of a number of repairs we did to help the house sell faster and for more money than if we hadn't made the repairs before putting it on the market.

Collect a number of these "small" assets, and you may find that you've covered many estate costs, thereby preserving more money for the beneficiaries (which hopefully includes you) and increasing the amount of the estate. These could cover an executor commission of 1–3%, if you choose to take one and/or are legally entitled to one (depending on state law).

Disclaimer: I am the fastidious executrix who claimed an $8 refund on a canceled magazine subscription; a $26 refund (times two!) on that fiscal quarter's long-term care premium (alas, a policy that was paid for but never used by my parents); and an $18 refund on my father's E-Z Pass account. Obsessive? Or crazy like a fox? You be the judge.

## Plug the Leaks

Eliminate estate "leaks" when you have a moment. These tiny, recurring charges may seem insignificant when you have much larger fish to fry regarding the estate. However, even small charges add up over time. Once you have taken care of the truly urgent matters, take an afternoon to cancel magazines, newspapers, and other mail and electronic subscriptions. (You can identify many of them by reviewing a recent credit card bill.) Consider canceling unneeded services and/or utilities (such as cable TV) to reduce monthly bills, charges, and debits to the estate.

The average estate is open for longer than one year. With twelve months in every year, you'll soon realize that a $39 monthly charge quickly becomes costly. Plug these kinds of leaks, and you'll preserve more of the estate for the beneficiaries (who will love you for it).

## Dear Estate Diary ...

Right about now, you're likely saying to yourself, "There is no freakin' way that I can remember all of these estate details! What I have taken care of already and what is still yet to do ..." Exactly. That's why I recommend that you get a simple, spiral-bound notebook or lined agenda to use as an estate journal. Keep all of your estate-related notes in this one place, and it will save you hours of labor. Why reinvent the wheel each time you find yourself with a few hours during which to work on estate matters? Simply refer back to your estate journal and pick up where you left off.

Make the journal one that suits your needs. Silly as it sounds, only write on one side of each page—I learned this when I was trying to flip over pages while simultaneously holding a cell phone in my other hand. As a starting point for your own estate journal, document the date on which the action took place; summarize conversations you've had by company name and representative; write down phone numbers for easy reference; and record amusing things as well as important discoveries. (The amusing things don't serve a legal purpose; they simply add a note of levity to what can be a lengthy process. Or, you can make a book out of it someday! Just not this year, please—I need all of the book sales that I can get.)

Here is a sample page from an estate journal:

6/12/2018 - called XYZ Bank at 800-555-1212 re:
CD #4050000; spoke with Carol; she said to send letter
addressed to her at bank address; include original
death certificate plus letter requesting that account be
closed and check made out to Estate of My Loved One

6/13/2018 - spoke with estate attorney; he said deadline to
convert IRAs into inherited IRAs is July 2018

6/15/2018 - received refund check for $501.45 from GGG Auto
Insurance for unused policy period; deposited into estate
bank account

6/17/2018 - called SSA at 800-555-1212; informed them that My
Loved One continues to receive Social Security deposits despite
a death notice being filed last month; they assured me that
they will file a Notice of Reclamation to pull back this
month's deposit from account; no need for action on my
part; confirm on monthly bank statement

☼ **The estate journal serves as your personal assistant during the estate administration process. With everything recorded in one place, you will never be at a loss for a name, phone number, or asset status.**

Your estate diary helps you keep track of everything in one place. There are just too many estate details for you to remember, so don't bother: write it all down. You don't want to finally get through the touch-tone phone chain after waiting on hold with a financial institution for an hour and then be asked, "What is the account number?" or "Can I have the deceased's SSN?"

As you panic, the word "um" comes out of your mouth, and you frantically run about the room, trying to find the piece of paper that has the information on it. Don't be the "um" person: have the information close at hand and be the all-star executor that you know you are.

## Get to Know More About: Mary

Speaking of all-stars, my mother was a person who possessed a staggering degree of both efficiency and creativity. Our parents did not become parents easily. In fact, my brother wasn't born until almost four years after our parents married, despite the fact that my mother wanted kids, <u>many</u> kids, right away. I believe the number was ten (at least that's what she told me years later)! But after she pushed out ten-pound Tom, of which nine pounds was his head, she reduced that number.

Our parents told me that they were so darn fascinated by my brother that they pretty much stopped watching television after he was born and just put him in the center of the room and stared at him. They were so distracted by the sheer wonder of my brother that I somehow slipped into the picture 17 months later. It took another five years after my birth for Terry to come along.

With all of the time it took to build her family, my mother was very excited to stop working and to become a stay-at-home mom. It was a real luxury to have a mother waiting at the front door when we came home from school each day. But she used the hours that we were at school well.

She was pretty good at making Halloween costumes for us each year, but one year she outdid herself. She created Tom's costume out of blue fabric and cardboard, and suddenly he was "Jaws" rising from the deep as seen on the iconic movie poster—complete with blood-stained mouth. I was to be a birthday party (yes, a concept, not just a thing), which included a cardboard table with tablecloth, plates, cups, and flatware glued to each place setting at the table, and a cardboard "cake" with eye holes as the centerpiece. Mind you, this is before the Internet, so there were no inspirational postings or designs to follow.

On another occasion, I went to elementary school one morning and came home six hours later to a newly repainted and wallpapered bedroom.

My mother, beaming: "Do you like it?? Huh??"

Me: "Um … okay … but … I don't really like pink."

My mother: [sigh]

## Things to Consider:

☐ *Do your best to identify financial documents, in both paper and electronic form, as you go through the home.*

☐ *Do not dispose of any documents at this time; you cannot immediately discern what is a lead and what is not.*

☐ *Reduce recurring monthly charges to the estate if they are unnecessary.*

☐ *Start, and use, an estate journal to keep track of what you've done and what you still need to do on the estate.*

### Chapter Six

# THE WIDE, WIDE WORLD OF IMPORTANT DOCUMENTS

## Can Safe-Deposit Boxes Be <u>Too</u> Safe?

The issue of safe-deposit boxes is not one I had ever considered prior to my parents' deaths. I have since learned that the problem with them is that it practically requires an act of Congress to open them … and that's if you have the key! I distinctly recall walking into the local branch of my parents' bank, death certificates and safe-deposit key in hand.

This was a week or two after the funeral, and I had both death certificates, my letters testamentary, and the safe-deposit key. (The key, of course, doesn't have the name of the bank on it; however, my extensive investigative training—not to mention conveniently finding the bank statement with the annual charge for the box on it—allowed me to deduce the location.) Despite all of my proof, the bank officer initially met my request with skepticism. I had to jump through a number of additional hoops in order to access the box.

Once I had met the burden of proof to their high standard, I was led into a small room in which to review the contents of the box, alone. I have a creative imagination, which, coupled with the lack of closure and inability to say goodbye to my parents, raised my expectations as to what might be in the box. Would there be a letter to us from our parents? A surprise stash of cash? Documentation indicating that they were descended from a prominent European family? No, no, and no. In fact, the contents were uniformly dull and disappointing. They included:

- My father's transcript from Villanova University (3.44 – nice work, Bart) and his diploma
- Documentation of post-graduate courses he later took through George Washington University and the New School for Social Research (OK, didn't know that …)
- 1970 closing and mortgage documents for my parents' then-current home in Parsippany, New Jersey
- 1967 closing and mortgage documents for their prior home in Framingham, Massachusetts (no longer owned by them)
- 1963 closing and mortgage documents for their first home in New City, New York (um, I think it's okay to shred those)
- Documents from my father's service in the U.S. Marine Corps, his rank, and discharge papers
- Birth and baptismal certificates for us kids
- Re-issued birth certificates for both parents, dated 1987, which I suspect they obtained in order to get passports to visit me during my junior year abroad at the Université de Nice, France
- My parents' birth and marriage certificates
- A handwritten list on lined paper, circa the early 2000s, in which my mother denoted whom she wished to receive specific items, like jewelry and music boxes.

The last was the most interesting document of the whole lot! Although it hadn't been updated for a number of years, this was the one item that held insight into my mother's thoughts and wishes. A bequest of a specific music box from her collection to a neighbor. A different music box to a close colleague at The Seeing Eye in Morristown, New Jersey, where my mother worked in development in her 60s and 70s. A note that I should receive the diamond ring that my mother wore as the replacement for her original engagement ring and wedding band, both of which were stolen from our home in the 1970s when we all went in the station wagon to a drive-in movie.

Oops.

We had buried our parents with their wedding rings. Our logic was simple: our father had worn his simple, silver band since he had put it on in 1961, and our mother had utilized this replacement ring as a stand-in for the ones that were taken. It made sense that they should have them in their final resting place. Had it been an expensive diamond ring, we might have reconsidered. But it was not, so we did not.

As I said, oops. Good to know, two weeks too late.

I wasn't tremendously upset by this oversight. As with life, everything depends on timing. I doubt most executors will have the opportunity (or the proof documents!) to access their loved one's safe-deposit box in the three days between a death and the funeral. If you do, wonderful—more power to you! If, like me, this is not a possibility, so be it.

## These Documents Are Part of Your Life

I spoke in an earlier chapter about your initial pass through the home to identify the documents most urgently needed in advance of the wake, funeral, and burial: those that specifically relate to your loved one's final wishes and their thoughts regarding their own plans. I also spoke about financial documents and all those that relate to identifying and collecting your loved one's assets (after the funeral, of course). I consider all of these to be important documents unless, and until, they are definitively proven NOT to be important.

I receive many questions regarding retention of important documents in relation to an estate. This is early in the estate administration process to be talking about what to keep and what to shred, so for now, keep it all. You are still reeling from your loved one's death, and you are not yet fully versed as to what will or will not be required for claim and tax purposes. So don't use your emotional energy at this time to determine what can be disposed of. There will be time for that later.

However, before I proceed further, let me just state that you should never, ever get rid of wills, trust documents, powers of attorney, proof of authority, or birth/marriage/adoption/death certificates (and no, scanning them is not sufficient for court purposes). Can you guarantee that you will find all of your loved one's assets while the estate is open? No? Neither can I, and I do this for a living. So keep it all. It takes comparatively little room in your home in relation to its potential importance. If you'd like to argue this point with me in a bar sometime, feel free. But know in advance that I'm right.

☼ **Important documents are called that for a reason: they are important. Do not shred them. Do not burn them. Do not dispose of them. They serve as both proof and history, and they do not lose their value over time.**

## Setting Up Your Initial Files

You may ask, "Where do I store all of this paper?" Excellent question, audience. As I mentioned, your first storage spot will be a box or shopping bag to remove the documents from your loved one's home and bring them into your own. Once you have some downtime, and you have the luxury of reviewing the documents more closely, you will want to organize them.

I like to use a banker's box with hanging file folders, writing the subject or vendor name on the file tab. Low-cost, low-tech, and uber-portable, this solution fits the vast majority of estates. As a professional organizer and super-nerd, I alphabetize the folders and use a label maker to label each file. But if that's not in your makeup, don't stress about it. Just be sure that, at a glance, you can find the file you need. When the life-insurance company returns your call and asks for your loved one's policy number, you want to be able to find it right away!

For example, I drop paid electric bills into the utility folder as I find them; medical receipts into that folder (remember, you are looking for deductions as well as assets); bank statements into that bank's folder. Set it up once, and it will aid you (and your estate attorney) throughout the whole process, whether administering the estate takes six months or six years.

You will likely find that the documents cover a range of years, and your assumption may be to retain only the latest documents. I would caution you to resist the temptation to do so, for a number of reasons. First off, you may need to know how a particular asset was initially funded. Or, you may need to determine Date of Death value (if much time has passed between your loved one's passing and your administration of the estate). You may also need to know how many years have passed since an investment occurred. Put the documents in each folder in chronological order if you have time, but don't shred anything just yet.

Hold onto your banker's box for the requisite number of years after the estate closes (not the date that your loved one passed away!). You can consult with your estate attorney and/or CPA as to how many years that might be for your state and your situation. You might locate additional assets or need to provide documentation to tax authorities over the next few years. Eventually, you can reduce the number of documents that you retain, with the exception of those important documents we discussed earlier.

## Things to Consider:

- ☐ *Determine whether your loved one held a safe-deposit box and, if so, access it as soon as is reasonable.*
- ☐ *Set up an easy filing system for estate documents.*
- ☐ *Retain estate documents for the requisite number of years after the estate closes.*
- ☐ *Permanently retain essential documents including wills, death certificates, and proof-of-authority papers.*

## Chapter Seven

# GETTING TO KNOOOOOW YOU, GETTING TO KNOW ALL ABOUT YOU [FROM *THE KING AND I*]

## The Things They Keep

Admittedly, I am not your material-possessions girl when it comes to estates—I'm your assets girl. (Many of my fellow professional organizers, however, do focus on helping seniors downsize or helping children empty their parents' homes.) Despite the fact that stuff is not my specialty, I have had the experience of emptying a fully-occupied, four-bedroom, full-basement, attic-in-the-house-and-the-garage, suburban home, and I feel your pain. We acquire so much in our lives, which is further compounded if your loved one lived in the same residence for a long time (say, 42 years, give or take a month). As humans, if we have no real incentive to pare down, we tend not to do so.

My parents had a nice home, but they had long ago stopped regularly "sifting" through their belongings. They intended to do so when it came time to move to a smaller, retirement home. Or, at least, that is what I tell myself. I distinctly recall a conversation I had with my mother a year or so before my parents' unexpected deaths.

For the last several years of their lives, my parents had hired me to serve as their biweekly cleaning lady, and I had spent every other Saturday morning at their house taking care of the bigger cleaning jobs to work in conjunction with their own daily maintenance. Often, if I finished early, I would ask (beg) my parents if I could address a "problem" area of their home—say, a single closet or a corner of the full basement. You know, just to get a jump on it for the eventual day when they planned to move.

No, they always said, there's no need. We'll get to it someday. (Just so you know, "someday" exists neither in time nor place and not on any physical plane or in any alternate reality. It's like every time I ask Eddie if we can get a dog, and he answers, "We'll see." Ain't never gonna happen, folks.)

But once, when I cornered my mother in her office (a.k.a., my brother's old bedroom) to ask if I could please, please, *please* work on just one closet out of the six in the home, she gave me a different answer to the question. "Don't worry, you'll have the chance to go through everything while handling our estates when we're gone." And then she laughed. Not a sinister laugh or an evil laugh, but rather a bemused laugh, as if she could already picture me on my hands and knees, going through dusty boxes and sorting rusty tools. So when I was working in the house by myself after their deaths, doing that very thing, I couldn't help but alternately smile at the memory of her amusement and curse my parents for not addressing some of the stuff sooner.

Admittedly, some of the items I found were charming: a few blank thank-you cards that my mother had left over from her bridal shower in 1961; a few invitations that my mother had left over from *my* bridal shower in 2010; a grainy black-and-white photo of my father's favorite dog from his childhood; extra souvenirs from the many vacations they took in their final years (thank YOU for the Slovenian salt flower, Mary!).

Some of the items were less charming… say, for example, the 123 tennis balls I found in the garage. My father had run marathons throughout his 40s and 50s and only stopped after having hip-replacement surgery. He then switched to walking the neighborhood, including circumnavigating our old high school up the street. As he walked the grounds, he would pick up change, occasional dollar bills, and tennis balls that had been hit over the fence around the school courts.

He began bringing the tennis balls home. For years. I once asked him why he took these tennis balls, and he explained, "I don't know … I might need them someday to throw around with a dog [we never got one] or to play with my grandkids." Hmm. Did he expect to roll tennis ball after tennis ball to my nieces, for hours of endless fun?? In the end, each and every lint-covered ball went into the dumpster.

Laugh if you will at this image, but I fully expect that each person reading this will encounter their own version of a tennis ball collection in their loved one's estate.

Allow me to make a note here regarding your loved one's books. For many people, that is the collection they will encounter that takes up the most amount of space and weight. Yes, you can donate books in good shape to your local library, but even they don't want textbooks, reference books, old magazines, and the like (always call first or check their website for donation restrictions). Regardless of whether you sell or donate these tomes, always, always flip through all books for hidden cash, photos, or letters. It takes just a few seconds per book and could result in a real find with financial or sentimental value.

# Don't Enter the Basement Alone: A Tale of Seven Deaths

Frankly, the ground and second floors of my parents' house weren't really that bad in terms of furniture, décor, and other items. I have been in many homes, and my parents' place was easily one of the better ones among people in their age group. There is, however, the matter of the basement, which embodied the "out of sight, out of mind" adage perfectly.

The basement had been an open, cinderblock-walled, cavernous space when I was little, but then my parents "finished" it in the late 1970s. They chose an attractive, gray wood paneling, had carpet installed, and opted for a storage area under the stairs to reduce clutter. They also sectioned off the utilities with a wall and folding-door combination, set up an exercise area on one side of the stairwell, and a TV-viewing, Atari-playing area with a sofa on the other side. It was an excellent use of a large amount of space and a great way to give our five family members different places to hang out (and/or get away from each other).

This same excellent use of space became a not-so-excellent place to put things which my parents didn't want to deal with at the moment. A collection of moments had added up to a lifetime of clutter. And, as I found out, much of it was inherited clutter.

A good portion of the basement contained things that my father didn't want to get rid of—newspaper clippings of his race times; handwritten pads of financial projections, an example of FORO (Fear Of Running Out, as opposed to millennials' FOMO, Fear Of Missing Out); five tiles from a long-ago bathroom renovation. But, part of the basement was consumed by things that my parents themselves had inherited when their own parents (and my mother's brother) passed away. So when I went down to the basement, I thought it was to sort out things from two estates (my parents'). Little did I know that I would be doing the hard work they hadn't done on five *other* estates. That makes seven. Oy.

Nothing down there was valuable, per se, but there were points of interest among the boxes and piles: some old black-and-white photos of generations past; a scrapbook of poetry that I originally assumed had been written by my grandfather but only recently determined was actually my great-grandfather's!; a pair of Hummel figures that I recall sitting on a shelf in my maternal grandparents' country kitchen.

All in all, it was the flotsam and jetsam of estates: old metal (not silver) tea sets, at least four sets of old (not silver) flatware, Christmas cards from people whose names we cannot remember and their children's names even less so, and a hodgepodge of other items for which we could find no home and no purpose.

I am darn proud that the cardboard boxes won't be passed down to yet another generation. I sold, donated, gave away, or recycled the vast majority of the items. I learned about metals recycling (ah, if we had only had copper!); I learned about the fragility of paper documents and old photos; I learned that there is such a thing as having too much Tupperware and too many old cookie tins. And I learned why my parents had never addressed this space while they were alive. Smart people, that Bart and Mary ...

## The Law of Physics as It Relates to an Estate

If you are considering moving everything from your deceased loved one's home into *your* home out of "tribute" to their memory, don't. Just don't. It is a law of physics that two solid objects cannot occupy the same space at the same time. Roughly interpreted, that means that there is no way in heck that you can fit another household into your own. Nor should you want to. And don't even talk to me about renting a storage unit for the next umpteen years!

There is no need to feel guilty for not keeping everything your loved one owned. Their things were not part of them, and they should be used and enjoyed by the living—but that doesn't mean it has to all stay with you. What to take, then? Those items that hold the most meaning for you or that you can use happily in your own home. Your loved one doesn't want you to feel the weight of everything they owned during their lifetime. Use and appreciate what fits the way you live, have your relatives do the same, and then sell/donate/recycle what is left so that it can be used and appreciated by someone else. Circle of life, my friends. Don't make me break into a song from *The Lion King*.

A note regarding charitable donations: Dispose of anything broken, stained, or otherwise damaged. Thrift shops do not want them either. By donating them, you are merely gumming up the works of their fundraising operations.

A commonly suggested solution when you're having trouble relinquishing an object is to take a photo of any item that reminds you of your loved one but that you cannot keep. The images can be stored on your phone or computer for reference, while the actual object can be put to better use by someone else.

If you are struggling with what to keep and what to toss/sell, you may wish to hire a professional organizer to facilitate the process. Sometimes an impartial third party can provide you with a safe space (and some clarity) in which to reasonably view your loved one's belongings. There are any number of charities that could better use the furniture, clothes, tools, and renovation materials left behind. Make someone's day while making room!

## THE PHOTOS [Cue Dramatic Music Here]

If there is anything that can quickly derail the administration of an estate, it is the discovery of a huge cache of photos. It starts off innocently enough: you take a quick glance at an album, then start to paw through a photo box, then the next thing you know, you're fully ensconced on the sofa going through EVERY photo there. When you look up, darkness has fallen, and you've missed two meals. That is the power of the family photo.

On the positive side, finding a photo that you've never seen before is like a small gift. Each shot reveals a side of your loved one that you may not have known about, especially if the photos are from their younger years. You're going to want to give these photos time and attention.

Now is not the time. Carefully gather all of the albums and loose photos and bring them to your home for later perusal. These photos have no time limit, whereas other matters from the estate do. It gives you something to look forward to when the hard work is done—perusing the photos while holding a Bart-sized glass of wine (read on).

## Get to Know More About: Bart

My father was an athlete in his youth and early twenties, and he became an athlete again when he hit 40 and joined the long-distance running craze that was then at its height. But even in those in-between years and the later years, he had an interest in health and nutrition. And he was pretty much on point as to the knowledge that he acquired by reading and which he then applied.

My earliest recollection of "Healthy Eating Dad" was when I was a little kid, sitting at our kidney-shaped, Formica kitchen table, eating my breakfast cereal (something decidedly *not* healthy). My father had his supersized bowl of Chock Full of Oats and Barley, and he added even *more* fiber by sprinkling a spoonful of wheat germ on top. Then he looked over at me and proceeded to sprinkle a spoonful of wheat germ on MY sugary bowl of cereal. Most kids would have reacted at that point, but not me. I am the middle child and simply accepted the wheat germ as a *fait accompli*.

Dad eventually learned about Scandinavian crispbread (as an alternative to white bread), the benefits of prunes (I won't elaborate here), salmon as an excellent source of omega-3s (way before the rest of the country heard about it), and the all-important heart benefits of a glass of red wine with dinner. In fact, he internalized the value of wine so well that he may have overdone it. Instead of a normal wine glass, he would use the largest goblet commercially available and fill it up to the top for his "one" glass of red wine with dinner.

Now, whenever my husband or I overfill a wine glass (above an "acceptable" portion), we accuse the other of pouring a "Bart-sized glass of wine." (Full disclosure: We do not then pour it back into the bottle. We go ahead and drink it. Apparently, it is an inherited trait.)

## Things to Consider:

- [ ] *View your loved one's possessions with a sociologist's eye!*
- [ ] *Take what you can reasonably use, and love, in your own home and with your current lifestyle.*
- [ ] *Donate / sell / recycle everything else, without guilt.*
- [ ] *Secure the photos, but do not focus on them at this time.*

## Chapter Eight

# SAVE ON LEGAL COSTS BY DOING MUCH OF THE WORK YOURSELF

### You're a Bargain, You

Depending on their experience and what part of the country you live in, estate attorneys typically charge by the quarter-hour, with the average hourly rate for the attorney being $250–$400 and a reduced rate of $150–$200 for tasks done by a paralegal on their staff. I'll give you a minute to get up off the floor … Anyway, you may now realize that there is a definite advantage to taking on some of the administrative work yourself.

Be upfront with your estate attorney: indicate that you plan to do much of the hands-on work yourself (gathering documents, identifying assets, writing claim letters), but that you will rely on his/her guidance and expertise regarding legal matters, filing dates, reporting requirements, and the like.

Update the estate attorney regularly, but task him/her only with those questions you can't answer or do yourself. Remember, these are billable hours. If you do have questions that require the attorney's action, save money by trying to group them into a single email rather than ten separate ones. This way, the estate attorney can focus on your loved one's estate for a solid hour instead of multiple, 15-minute blocks over the course of a week.

## Create an Estate Spreadsheet

This can be done either on paper or on a computer, although with the computer you have the added advantage of automatically calculating column totals. Use this spreadsheet to track identified assets, claim forms submitted, and assets received. It should include what assets you've identified to date, that asset's account or policy number, estimated date-of-death value, whether you've sent in the claim forms (and on what date), and how much has been received in payments into the estate account.

Once you set up your spreadsheet, run it by your estate attorney to ask whether there are any additional columns you should add, depending on the circumstances surrounding the estate or trust.

Here is a sample assets spreadsheet:

| Company Name | Asset Type | Account/ Policy Number | DOD Amount | Claim Submitted | Asset Received |
|---|---|---|---|---|---|
| XYC Bank | CD | 8765433219 | $5,697.25 | 10/7/18 | 12/5/18 |
| T&T Securities | IRA | 56-7784320 | $27,888.00 | 10/22/18 | |
| Town Newspaper | Refund | 3178 | $13.45 | 10/22/18 | 11/30/18 |
| Credit Union | Savings Acct | 9990456 | $40,140.26 | 10/25/18 | 12/11/18 |

In this example, I've included "DOD Amount" to represent the amount the asset was worth on the Date of Death of your loved one. There is a common misconception that if you simply let the asset slide for a few months (or years), you will be able to claim the increased interest. Sadly, this is not true for the majority of assets (note: it does vary from state to state). Have a Certificate of Deposit with a bank that is now worth $5,725.13? Sorry, Charlie—the estate will receive the $5,697.25 that the CD was worth the day your loved one passed away. Rode a stock-market wave that increased your loved one's IRA by 12% because you failed to notify the bank of your loved one's death? Odds are, they will not let you collect that increased value, but rather what the account was worth on your loved one's DOD. As always, you may wish to consult with your estate attorney about the proper time to submit a claim for an asset. But the general answer will be, "As soon as you get a chance to do so." There is rarely value in delaying.

If you are dealing with an exceptionally complex estate—numerous assets held in different states, for example—or are handling multiple estates at one time, you may wish to create a spreadsheet for debits as well as one for assets. We spoke about using the check register for the estate bank account as a way to track payments out of the account. For the vast majority of estates, this will be sufficient. However, for that small percentage of complex estates, a debit spreadsheet may be essential for your benefit and that of your estate attorney and tax preparer.

I have a client for whom the debit spreadsheet is an absolute necessity. The trust account is paying for ongoing expenses in relation to multiple properties out of state. It is unlikely that you will need to do this (utilizing the two check registers for my parents' estate accounts sufficed when I was serving as executrix), but if it helps you, by all means, do so.

## The Estate Account: The Spring You Return to Again and Again

Pay all debts out of, and deposit all assets into, the estate/trust bank account. Consider the estate account as your one-stop shop for income and expenses. Everything is there, at a glance, with a running total so that you know where you stand at any given moment. Resist the urge to pay small bills out of your own bank account; it's easier to pay them once out of the estate account rather than write the checks out of your personal account and then reimburse yourself later (doubling your work and muddying the waters). Believe me: don't complicate what doesn't need to be complicated.

At the risk of sounding like a broken record, I urge you to maintain a detailed check register of money coming in and going out. I find that the online log of bank activity doesn't allow you to denote many details, so I much prefer the low-tech, eminently-practical, paper check register. At year's end, you can photocopy the register pages to provide to the individual or company preparing the estate's tax returns.

Remember: Good recordkeeping is essential for an executor, for both tax and legal reasons. Manage the estate account correctly the first time, and you won't have to do it again amidst all of the other duties you have as executor. As an added bonus, this written record helps maintain transparency with the beneficiaries, thereby decreasing the chances that they will accuse you of creative accounting. When it's all there in black and white, there is very little to argue over.

## Things to Consider:

- ☐ *Handle as many of the administrative tasks as you feel comfortable doing.*

- ☐ *Keep your estate attorney informed on a regular basis.*

- ☐ *Create an estate spreadsheet to track assets that have been identified, claimed, and collected.*

- ☐ *Use the estate bank account to pay all estate expenses and to collect all estate assets.*

**Chapter Nine**

# A POCKET GUIDE TO IDENTIFYING ASSETS

## The Encyclopedia of Estate Assets

You didn't start reading this book to get bogged down in innumerable details about possible asset situations that don't apply to 95% of estates. Allow me to focus on the types of assets you are most likely to encounter, saving you both time and mental exhaustion.

Assets come in many forms. Here is a very brief list of assets you may encounter or should at least be aware of while doing your search for paper and electronic documents:

- Checking and savings accounts at banks and credit unions

- Certificates of deposit and money market accounts

- Deeds and mortgage documents

- Stock, bond, and other investment funds

- Life insurance policies

- Death and dismemberment policies

- Annuities with a payable-upon-death benefit

- IRAs, both traditional and Roth

- Pensions that include a payable-upon-death benefit

- Long-term care policies with a payable-upon-death benefit

- Vacation homes or timeshares

- Health Savings Accounts

- Organization memberships with payable-upon-death benefits

- Military records (your loved one's service may provide a benefit)

- Royalties and dividends

- Vehicles, including cars, trucks, motorcycles, and boats

- Refund checks

- Account overpayments

- Oil and gas revenues

- Taxicab medallions ...

All right, I've gotten into the weeds a bit here. Anyway, you have already gathered and reviewed every document in your loved one's home that is not clearly recycling. You have put all of these documents into your banker's box, and at some point (perhaps while watching a home-renovation marathon on TV), you have sorted them into categories to get a handle on what you have.

You have additionally followed the leads you found in the house and those you've gleaned from conversations with your loved one while they were alive. If they mentioned their investments, if they complained about poor interest rates on their certificates of deposit, if they talked about land they inherited from a relative—these are all leads.

You have continued to open and review your loved one's mail that has now been coming directly to your own home. End-of-year mail is especially useful for determining where your loved one kept their assets. Tax statements arriving in December and January are the most valuable documents you will find. Increasingly, many investments, bank accounts, etc. are fully managed online except for end-of-year tax statements.

Find and review copies of prior-year tax returns. This will save you many hours of searching for possible assets and will also help the estate attorney and tax professional when preparing current year taxes. More importantly, an asset reported on last year's tax return is a direct lead to claiming it following your loved one's passing.

There are additional sources of information that can lead you to assets owned by your loved one. In my exhaustive review of my parents' basement, I found the Definitive Collection of Every Check Ever Written by Mary and Bart. In other words, I found scores of check registers from their bank accounts going back decades. It's all there: the checks to the orthodontist for three sets of braces; the checks to various universities to get us educated; the "equalization" checks in which my mother settled up with the other two kids after one child received some financial benefit. Aside from the guilt incurred by the realization that, "Wow, I was expensive to raise!", it is an easy transition to view our parents' check registers as a history of their love for us. You can be sure that I won't be shredding those anytime soon.

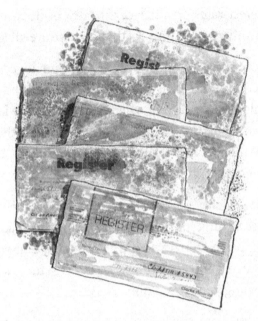

I also used the registers as an additional source of information for my parents' investments and policies. Because my parents recorded both online transfers as well as checks that they physically wrote out (a habit that I continue with my own accounts), I could see where all their income went. This was a way to ensure that I had, indeed, identified all of their assets.

## Death and Taxes

One of the great things about dying is that you yourself are not responsible for paying taxes after you die. You, as the dead person, get a pass. Your executor, however, IS responsible for using the estate to pay any taxes you might owe.

Although surprising to many people, your executor will have to file a final personal tax return for you in the year that you die. I am forever grateful to my parents, who passed away in early May, for having taken care of the prior year's tax return instead of asking for an extension. For subsequent years, you and your (new-best-friend) estate attorney will be concerned with filing estate tax returns.

We are fortunate that death taxes are not as burdensome as they used to be. The federal limit is now over $5 million, below which estate taxes are not incurred. Very few of us have to worry about having an estate valued at more than $5 million. Most states have fairly generous limits: some run in tandem with the federal limit, while many others don't kick in until the estate exceeds $1 million. Remember: your estate attorney and/or CPA will be deducting a number of expenses from your loved one's estate (including their own substantial fees), so the final estate tax bill may be appreciably smaller once all costs are factored in.

Not long ago, however, death taxes kicked in at lower asset levels. For example, back in 2012 (when my parents passed away), the state of New Jersey had an estate tax that kicked in at $675,000. (Note: Fortunately, New Jersey increased that amount a few years after my parents' deaths.) For those who live in the northeastern United States, $675,000 is very easy to meet when you factor in a home valued at $400,000–$500,000, a few IRAs, and some additional savings. New Jersey is one of only six states that also imposes an inheritance tax, so residents of the Garden State face a double whammy in death taxes. (This is why we all move out a few years prior to dying.)

Inexplicably, we are all surprised by taxes every year. It's rare that a taxpayer says, "Oh, I fully expected to owe xxx dollars to the IRS/state this year." Usually, when the return shows an amount due rather than a refund, our reaction falls somewhere between disbelief and rage. Considering that it is basic math, we shouldn't be so surprised. And yet we are.

I recall the glorious year that my mother entered a contest with chocolatier Godiva and won. The year was 2001, and it was magical. My mother won the grand prize—a year's worth of Godiva's products. You have to realize that we Moynahans are chocoholics, so this was akin to a heroin addict let loose in an opium field. The joy! The delirium! Every month, for twelve months, my mother received a shipment of Godiva wares averaging one pound: one pound of dark chocolate squares, one pound of Godiva hot chocolate, one pound of Godiva ice cream, etc. My mother willingly shared her bounty, so we all benefited from her good luck.

And then the year-end tax statements started to arrive. One day in the mail, my mother received a 1099-Misc (miscellaneous income) with $750 listed in the "other income" field. She was apoplectic. "What," she bellowed, "I have to pay tax on my prize?!?!" This was followed by a stream of words that verged very close to profanity. It had never occurred to her that the value of the prize would be added to their other earnings from my father's pension, Social Security, and her part-time job. She almost (almost) regretted the win that year, but then memories of the milky-smooth treats we had all enjoyed calmed her from her frenzy.

## Things to Consider:

- [ ] *Identify all possible assets in your loved one's name.*
- [ ] *Use prior tax returns and check registers to tease out other possible assets, including those managed online.*
- [ ] *Remember: You will have to file estate tax returns as long as the estate is open.*

## Chapter Ten

# REACH OUT AND TOUCH SOME ASSETS

## Begin the Claim Process

Identifying your loved one's assets is one thing; *claiming* them is another. On a positive note: come on, collecting money is fun! You have to admit there's a bit of a thrill every time a check comes in the mail, and you get to deposit it into the estate account. There is nothing more fulfilling than seeing that account balance inch upwards.

Inch is an apt word here. Although some assets will be relatively simple to claim, there are others that will require you to run the gauntlet before they come into your hands. Let me offer an example of a telephone conversation you might have when contacting a financial institution in an attempt to start the claim process.

After dialing the toll-free number, working your way through a phone tree, and saying the words "death claim" several times during the process, you will finally reach a live human being.

"Hello," you say. "I am the executor for my loved one's estate, and I'd like to determine whether you are holding any assets in his/her name."

"I'm so sorry for your loss. For verification purposes, can you please tell me the full name and Social Security number of your loved one?"

"Yes, it is [insert name of loved one] and [insert SSN]."

"Let me check … okay, so we'll first need to establish your authority as the rightful personal representative for your loved one. Can you please send us a letter and include an original death certificate as well as your proof-of-authority documents?"

"Sure, I can absolutely do that. But before I go through all of that trouble, can you let me know if my loved one even has assets with your company? The documents I found were pretty old."

"I'm so sorry, but I am not permitted to share that information until we confirm that you are authorized to receive this information."

"Okaaaaayyyyy … so I guess I'll send you that letter and documents, then."

"Thank you. Please be aware that it will take 6–8 weeks to process the documents before we can respond to you."

NOT KIDDING. This is the standard response you will get when you first begin the claim process. Try not to get upset with the poor customer service rep—they have a procedure that they must follow, and no amount of pleading will enable you to get around that. I have tried, and I have failed. Find your zen and anticipate this hurdle.

The format of your claim letter is not engraved in stone, but it must contain several important elements: your name, address, and contact information; your loved one's full name as well as some identifiers (SSN, date of birth, account or policy number); a death certificate (or copy) with the date of death; and your request (you want to know the account's value, you want to close the account, and you want a check sent to the estate, etc.). This can often be accomplished in the initial letter to the company, but sometimes you will be asked to send a follow-up letter with additional information.

Obviously, you are going to set up your standard claim letter and simply customize it for each vendor. There is no need to reinvent the wheel for each and every claim. Here's a sample go-by letter:

---

123 Smith Road
Anytown, NY 12345
November 2, 2018

ABC Bank
PO Box 55
Anytown, NY 12345

Account Owner:    [Deceased Loved One's Full Name]
Certificate of Deposit Number:  [Full Account Number]

To Whom It May Concern:

Thank you for your letter dated 10/20/2018, advising me how to begin the claim process for the assets held by [Deceased Loved One's Name]. As I previously informed you, [Deceased Loved One's Name] passed away in July 2018.

As the executor of [Deceased Loved One's Name]'s estate, I am responsible for taking care of his/her financial affairs. I have therefore enclosed the following documents:

- an original death certificate for [Deceased Loved One's Name];
- proof of my authority to act as executor for [Deceased Loved One's Name]'s estate;
- the completed claim form that your company sent me.

I have enclosed a self-addressed, stamped envelope for you to return the original death certificate once you have processed my claim.

Please let me know if you require any additional information to process this claim, both for the above-referenced Certificate of Deposit and any other accounts held by [Deceased Loved One's Name]. I thank you for your continuing assistance and support.

Sincerely,


[Executor's Typed Name]
[Executor's Phone Number]
[Executor's Email Address]

---

I recommend that you first call the company to request guidance as to how to proceed with a claim. I have found that the vast majority of companies are very receptive and, in fact, sympathetic when the next-of-kin calls following a death. This phone call accomplishes two tasks: 1) It usually results in a note being put into the company's system that your loved one has passed, making it easier for the subsequent customer service reps to know what's going on with the account; and 2) Very often the rep will provide you with the specific information they need to see in your letter.

Occasionally—very occasionally—a company will allow you to email the letter, scanned death certificate, and scanned proof-of-authority documents to them in lieu of mailing them. So scan your loved one's death certificate and your letters testamentary (or other court proof of your authority to act) and keep these on your computer for easy access.

You're going to need a lot of death certificates, so always ask if the company will accept a copy instead of an original.

☼ **If the company will accept it, send a copy of your loved one's death certificate instead of an original. If sending an original, always include a self-addressed, stamped envelope so that they may return it to you after the claim is processed.**

That's worth mentioning again: If sending an original death certificate, enclose a self-addressed, stamped envelope so that the company can return it to you after they've processed your claim. If you stagger your claims, you can reuse one death certificate multiple times.

As you successfully close an account and the check comes in, document the date and dollar amount on your asset spreadsheet and deposit the check into the estate/trust account. Do a short happy dance to congratulate yourself. Now move on to the next asset until you've claimed them all.

A note here regarding assets that are directly deposited into your loved one's account on a monthly basis. Social Security payments stop when the funeral home files your loved one's name and SSN as part of a death claim. (Be sure to confirm that the death claim "took"; my mother's immediately showed on her credit report, but my father's did not. A call to the Social Security Administration [SSA] rapidly corrected the oversight.) However, private pensions do not automatically stop! You must notify your loved one's former employer. And no, delaying that notification does not allow you to keep the money. You will have to pay it back in full.

If ever you doubted the efficiency of a government agency, allow me to assure you that the SSA is very, very good at stopping payments to the deceased. Should an extra payment slip through—as it did for one month for my father—they will slurp it back (as a former federal employee, yes, slurp is the official government term), without requiring any authorization on your part.

## Perfection is Overrated

Does all of this make you tense? Is your worry gene going into overdrive right about now? Breathe. We're not going for perfection here. As a recovering perfectionist myself, this was something I struggled with as I served as executrix for my parents. Our goal is PDG: "pretty darn good." Is it possible that you might overlook a small utility refund or another minor rebate? Yes. Is it a showstopper from an estate perspective? No. It's best to claim all assets while the estate is open, I agree. But there will be other opportunities to claim your loved one's assets.

Enter with me now the Realm of Lost Assets: those bits (or bags) of money that go unclaimed for years on end. Eventually, they are escheated (that's legalese for given) to a government bank account, most often to one in the state where the deceased was last known to live. Say there was a life insurance policy that your loved one purchased many moons ago and completely forgot about. You find no documentation in the home or in any of the mail that comes in after your loved one's death.

Years pass. You dutifully check for your loved one's name in online databases that list unclaimed assets throughout the country. Lo and behold, there is a listing for someone with your loved one's name at an unfamiliar address! You do further research and determine that this address is one where your loved one resided twenty years before their death. Since the holder company couldn't find your loved one after he/she moved, the company simply wrote it off, or "escheated" the asset and got it off their books. However, you are confident that this asset rightfully belongs to your loved one's estate.

In most cases, you can start the claim process online. You'll submit your claimant information to get the ball rolling. You will receive either a letter or email requesting further documentation that proves your claim to this asset. Here, we go back to the death certificate we maintained despite so many years passing (see—still needed!), as well as to the proof-of-authority documents for you to act as executor and/or beneficiary.

You may be asked to provide some proof connecting your loved one to the listed address; you may have to sign and have notarized an affidavit listing yourself and all other beneficiaries. As you work through this claim process over a period of months (or years), you are thankful for this discovery—goodness knows, the state or federal government would never have reached out to alert you about the asset—but you fervently wish that you had found this asset back when you were initially gathering the estate assets all those many years ago.

Yes, you may get another bite at the apple, but first you have to find the apple and then you have to *prove* that the apple is yours ... I mean, your loved one's. By the way, that apple hasn't grown over the years: in most cases, any interest earned on the apple after it was escheated has been going to the government, not added to the asset. So claim it now, before you yourself pass away and proving the rightful ownership of the asset passes to yet another generation of claimants.

## How to Divvy Up Your Own Kitty

Although this discussion falls more accurately under estate *planning* rather than estate *administration*, I want to address this issue with some food for thought. There are at least three schools of thought on how to divide your own assets in relation to your offspring: 1) Divide all assets even-Steven—à la Mary—between the children, without taking into consideration their individual financial circumstances; 2) Divide the assets according to each child's personal means; or 3) Divide the assets according to how much financial support each child has already received from you while you were alive.

In the first scenario, it is a simple question of math—divide the assets, once liquidated, by the number of children. This is the most common plan of action, as it is believed to be the one to cause the least strife among the children. However, that may not always be "fair" depending on individual circumstances. I distinctly recall the disagreement between my parents on that subject. Having named me as executrix, my parents wanted to make sure—years in advance—that I was aware of their wishes.

My mother emphatically insisted that I divide their assets three ways, with no exceptions or caveats. My father, who had served as an executor before, encouraged me to take the 1–3% fee allocated to personal representatives in their state. He knew firsthand how much work is involved in administering an estate and how many hours the executor will expend, uncompensated, in that pursuit.

When the time came to perform my duties, I was torn between following one or the other's advice. (Imagine one parent sitting on each shoulder, whispering in my ears!) In the end, I opted not to take the executor's fee and was only periodically annoyed at the cumulative amount of time (and many vacation days from work) that I spent identifying and collecting assets, distributing personal effects, and preparing the home for sale.

The second scenario is one employed by a percentage of parents but runs the risk of alienating the more affluent children. In effect, the parents are allotting a greater amount of assets to the child who chose a career path with a lower rate of remuneration. Attempting to "equalize" the financial situation of each child is fraught with difficulty at best and potentially disastrous at worst. Trying to compensate for each child's life choices with a greater or lesser inheritance is an exercise in frustration on all sides.

The final scenario is similar to the second, in which the parents try to make amends for any financial support they provided to their adult children beyond the normal costs of child-rearing. If the parents paid for college for all of the children but also covered the cost of medical school for one child, that is a huge financial discrepancy that the other children may or may not resent.

Other support—the gift of a car, covering rent for an adult child for an extended period, even covering the cost of a pricey wedding—can equally cause dissatisfaction among the children. My parents' personal philosophy during their lives was to "even up" at the time of the support: when they gave my brother their old car, my sister and I each received a check equivalent to the Blue Book value of the vehicle. In this way, they (successfully) alleviated any financial resentment between their children.

As with all decisions in estate planning, each choice must be made according to your personal circumstances. However, there is one recommendation that fits each and every situation: as parents, discuss your estate planning decisions with your adult children before your death. This way, the children can ask you any questions at that time. You want to avoid the situation in the estate attorney's office in which your children look on in shock (unless it's good shock) while the attorney explains the terms of your will.

If this is all too much, consider leaving everything to charity. The kids will forgive you ... eventually.

## Things to Consider:

☐ *Be patient with yourself and the financial institutions while claiming assets. It's not a fast process.*

☐ *Reuse the death certificates you have by utilizing a copy when possible and requesting the original back when required.*

☐ *Unclaimed assets will eventually be escheated to the government, but it takes years.*

☐ *Consider your own estate planning with your new knowledge in hand.*

## Chapter Eleven

# POTENTIAL PITFALLS TO AVOID WHILE ADMINISTERING AN ESTATE

## Groundhog Day

"If at first you don't succeed" … this should be the mantra of an executor. When dealing with paperwork and financial institutions, you'll need to be persistent. That means knowing what you sent to whom and when.

To help coordinate finances and requests, you should (as mentioned, but it's worth saying again) keep track of located assets AND expenses that have been paid during the administration of the estate. Many estate administration costs—including legal fees, estate organizer fees, and home repairs—can be deducted from the total value of the estate, thereby decreasing the estate's tax liability (if any).

As the executor, maintain regular contact with the beneficiaries. The more you update them (biweekly is recommended), the more you keep them in the loop and the more comfortable they'll feel. An added benefit? Once they see how much work you're doing, the beneficiaries are less likely to give you a hard time or to ask why it's taking so long. They can clearly see the sweat equity you are putting in to resolve the estate.

Don't be surprised if you mail a claim packet to a financial institution, but when you follow up to check on its status, they tell you they have no record of your request. It happens more often than you might think. I have a current client who has submitted documentation no fewer than three times to the same bank. So don't delete the letter off your computer and be prepared to send some a second or even third time. Incompetency happens.

Continue to open your loved one's mail that is now being forwarded directly to you. Forever, with a capital F.

Search for "unclaimed" assets in your loved one's name now and on an annual basis after the estate closes. Many assets won't be escheated for 10 or 15 years after the owner has passed. Check the unclaimed assets website for every state where your loved one resided; you should also check the national pointer databases in case an asset is being held in an unexpected state.

As mentioned, with very few exceptions, waiting to file for assets does NOT increase their value. I use the example of a bank CD: the interest does not continue to accrue the longer you wait. The claim value will be determined by your loved one's date of death, and that is what the estate will inherit no matter when you claim it.

Keep all estate documents, even after the estate is closed. Consult with your estate attorney and/or CPA as to when you can start shredding them. NEVER get rid of wills, power of attorney documents, or death certificates. And no—scanning them is not sufficient for legal purposes.

Although this is not a priority in the first few weeks after your loved one's death, you may eventually decide that the third-class mail you are receiving in their name is waaaaaay too much. To remove your loved one's name from direct-mail marketing, add their name to the Direct Marketing Association's Deceased Do Not Contact list at IMS-DM. com/cgi/ddnc. You must confirm receipt of an email after you complete the online form. This won't stop ALL mail coming to your loved one— companies with whom your loved one conducted business may still write—but it will greatly decrease the variety and volume of solicitations.

## The Glass Is Half Full

You may find estate work to be a contemplative opportunity. You will inevitably learn a lot about your loved one by going through all of their documents and belongings. Accept it as a gift and use that time to grieve, remember, and occasionally laugh.

I started this book by saying that I now consider my experience as executrix to my parents' estates to be a blessing, something that helped me to grow as a person as well as to grow closer to them. There is an intimacy that comes from administering an estate that you won't get from any other position. You are given tremendous responsibility but also almost exclusive access, in the absence of the person's physical presence. You have the opportunity to laugh with them as you carefully sort through the remnants of their life and discover (and re-discover) those things that made them special in the first place.

## Leave a Trail ...

It is hard to predict how or when you are going to leave this world for the next, so—like the stock market—don't try to time it. Give your executor a trail to follow once you're gone. If you don't want to do it in a formal fashion (carefully recording each detail in a special workbook or document), share your thoughts with them as these thoughts come to mind.

Hindsight is 20/20: I only realized after my parents were gone some of the jewels they had shared with me over the years. I specifically recall Mom giving me clues years in advance about their funerals and estates. One Saturday when I was there cleaning their house, my mother mentioned that she had attended a local talk about preparing to sell your home and that she was very impressed by the realtor who gave the presentation.

She handed me one of the realtor's cards (she kept the other) so that I could hire that specific realtor when it came time to sell their house. Not knowing what else to do with it, I dropped it in the hanging file titled "Mom & Dad's estates," in which I had already placed the contact information for their estate attorney and the deeds for their mausoleum plots. Another time, my mother brought home a hymn sheet from a funeral; she had loved how the choir sang it and decided then and there that she wanted it played someday at her funeral. So in that went to the file.

There were other tidbits thrown my way over the years, but these few particularly stuck out. What a great relief to pull out that hanging file a day after their deaths and be able to say, "Well, I don't know everything they would want, but I know **this**!" It makes for a small sense of security when your whole world is cut loose from its moorings.

## Things to Consider:

- ☐ *Document all assets and expenses.*
- ☐ *Keep in contact with all beneficiaries.*
- ☐ *Follow the trail of prior conversations with your loved one, then remember to leave your <u>own</u> trail for your eventual executor.*

# AMAZING GRACE

## The Thinnest Veil

To this day, I recall the sense of grace I felt in the days and weeks following my parents' deaths. It was as if the veil between life and death was thinnest during that time, like some portal between these two planes was left slightly ajar to enable me to make it through the first days and the funeral. If you ask me now, I would tell you that there is simply *no way* I could go through all of that again.

Only in retrospect can I see the tiny decisions made by our parents that collectively added up to an easier time for the three of us. I recall my mother explaining how she had selected their mausoleum slot solely for the comfort of visitors. The slot they chose had a bench nearby on which visitors could comfortably sit. Their crypt is at eye level so that we wouldn't have to strain our necks while sitting on that bench. Although there were open-air slots at the mausoleum, Mom insisted on an inside location so that weather wouldn't be a factor, and visitors could enjoy a climate-controlled environment. She chose a mausoleum section near a beautiful stained-glass window of Pentecost, with the Holy Spirit descending upon the disciples. A speaker system softly plays beautiful music. In return, we visit more often than we expected, taking advantage of all of the thoughtful touches our mother planned.

With some of the proceeds that we inherited from my parents, Eddie and I decided it would be good to buy a joint mausoleum slot on the same "block" as my parents. This way, relatives can visit four decedents for the price of one! Park once and you don't have to move your car. Of course, since my parents purchased during preconstruction, and we purchased several years after construction was completed, all of the prime locations were already sold. Our slot is closer to the ceiling, requiring an uncomfortable craning of the neck to read our names—as with all real estate: location, location, location.

I recall my sister and I visiting our parents' crypt a month after they were interred and wondering why there were no names, no lettering, nothing on the front of the mausoleum slot. There were just the temporary white labels that had been there on our last visit. We went to the mausoleum office to inquire, and it turns out that, although our parents had fully paid for their slot years before, they had not prepaid for lettering.

Terry and I had to pull out our credit cards to cover their names (do you realize how many letters are in Bartholomew??) as well as years of birth and death. We also added some tasteful bling so that they didn't appear to be loved less than some of their neighbors. Wanting to avoid this eventuality ourselves, Eddie and I have prepaid our names and years of birth, leaving just the cost of eight digits (years of death) for our survivors to cover!

One of the biggest things I recall from the days and weeks following our parents' deaths is that we were able to rely on the kindness of strangers (and friends). The words and actions of friends, family, work colleagues, and virtual strangers—all of what they did mattered. For all of you who had a kind word, who helped us in ways big and small, and whom I did not properly acknowledge or thank at the time, please know this: we remember, and we thank you from the bottom of our hearts. Following my own experience, I now make sure to send the card, to write on the remembrance page, to bake or send food, and to do my part to help the grieving. As I said, it all matters.

I owe tremendous gratitude to my brother and sister for staying both strong and classy throughout the process; in my line of work, I see families for which a tragic event like ours leads to ugly results. We are so very blessed that this drew us together instead of tearing us apart. I attribute much of that to Mary and Bart, but I also acknowledge our own choice to make that happen. I am so thankful for my in-laws (my new family) who showed up that terrible day and haven't left since, stepping up time and time again. I am grateful for all of our New York State Police and Drug Enforcement Administration colleagues, who were there both physically and emotionally for us during that time.

Thank you to Steve Priola for his compassion and for his creative solutions to our irregular wake requests. You and your staff at the Stephen J. Priola Parsippany Funeral Service took the weight off of us so that we could focus on saying goodbye to Mary and Bart.

I remember the woman at the Erie hotel who cried with me over the phone when I called to cancel my parents' reservation after they died. You didn't even know me, and you spontaneously shared in my grief. I am thankful for the friends who live far away yet who sent plants and flowers to soften the sting of death; we delighted in moving from arrangement to arrangement, reading the cards and discovering who had sent these lovely gifts. I appreciate the love and support that came from our faith communities and all that they did to ease our pain.

My family will never forget the caring and generosity of Jimmy and Torva Durkin, who supplied us with so much food from their Spring Street Deli in Ramsey, New Jersey, that I believe we have some in the fridge to this day. It made many a nice sandwich. Thank you to the friend who anonymously mowed our lawn while we were out making funeral arrangements. And thank you to the people I barely knew who sent emails and cards offering their support. Some continue to do so every anniversary of our parents' deaths, just to let us know that they remember, too.

When the estates were finally closed, I ordered silver necklaces from an Etsy seller in southern Spain with the Latin word *gratia* engraved on them for myself and my sister. I wanted to always remember the grace I received in the aftermath of the tragedy and that I continue to receive to this day.

## An Education and a Realization

It's hard to encapsulate everything I've learned since my parents' deaths. But one of the biggest things is definitely the fallacy of perfection. Maybe it's because I'm a middle child and an inveterate people-pleaser, but I always thought that a life well-lived involved perfection: a perfectly lived life, a perfectly managed career, a perfectly peaceful death. Yet, perfect is an unattainable goal for any mortal. So, I've had to revise my viewpoint and accept that I can't do anything perfectly.

I used to think that all of my character flaws destined me to a life of imperfection, and therefore, unhappiness. But I see, through my parents' lives, that a person can be imperfect and still be beautiful, loved, loving, and a positive influence on the world and those around them. And if it's true for my parents, then it must be true for me as well.

Just as there is no perfectly lived life, there can be no perfectly executed estate. How can an executor be expected—or expect of themselves—to be able to tie up every loose end their loved one leaves behind? Is there a way to conclude a life, tied with a bow? There isn't, so don't expect yourself to be able to do it for your loved ones, whether you serve as an executor once, twice, or a hundred times. You will always miss something. However, if you do it with love, you serve to honor the deceased as well as their life. And maybe that is what we should be striving for, however long it takes us to learn this lesson.

Even if it takes six and a half years of grieving to be able to put it all down on paper and to finally say:

Mom, Dad, I'm so sorry for the way you had to die. But I am so very grateful for the way you chose to live.

I love you, and I miss you — Eileen.

# APPENDIX

Please read the "Things to Consider" at the end of each chapter for an overview of the steps I take when administering an estate. These summaries serve as a quick reference guide so that you don't have to read the whole book again (although, would that really be so bad??). However, if you're lazy with a capital L …

## If You Read Nothing Else

I launched my estate organizing business in November 2016. Before I could even "open the doors," so to speak, I received a request from my sister, asking if I could provide some advice to her colleague who had just lost her mother. This colleague was understandably overwhelmed and was looking for some direction.

Here is a shortened version of the email that I wrote, from one sudden executrix to another. Hopefully, this summary will also help you get started.

"I am so sorry to hear of your mom's passing. You asked for some immediate guidance as to how to proceed. Here is a brief summary of my approach and philosophy.

An estate attorney will know how to proceed regarding legal questions (registering the executor with the county where your mother passed away; opening an estate/trust bank account; obtaining an EIN number for the estate; coordinating tax returns for the deceased individual and the estate; etc.).

My suggestions fall on the practical side of administering a loved one's estate.

1. Take care of first things first. Making funeral arrangements takes precedence over administrative matters.

2. Secure the home to the degree possible. Check doors, windows, and temperature settings; remove valuables; and use lights on timers.

3. Obtain an EIN number for the estate, set up an estate bank account, and get multiple death certificates (at least ten). An estate attorney can facilitate the first two; your funeral director will help with the third.

4. Identifying the deceased's assets and debts can be done by reviewing postal mail, documents already in the home, and email (if you can access the account).

5. Contact and make arrangements with utilities, newspaper delivery, and lawn/snow-removal services.

6. Have the estate attorney explain the terms of the will (if there is one).

7. Keep a single notebook in which to note dates, phone numbers, and the names of people you speak with at banks, brokerage houses, and other financial institutions.

8. Distill your loved one's belongings down to a reasonable amount; you can't keep it all.

Recognize that this is not a quick process, and that's OK."

# Resources

To find an estate attorney in your area, contact your state or local bar association—for example, New York's is NYSBA.org. However, your best resource for finding an excellent estate attorney will be your circle of friends and acquaintances. Chances are, if someone you respect had a good experience with an attorney, then you likely will as well.

To find a professional organizer (including yours truly!), go to the website for the National Association of Productivity and Organizing Professionals (NAPO) at NAPO.net. This organization, of which I'm a member and an officer in our local chapter, includes a wide variety of specialties. Mine happens to be estate administration, but the vast majority of members specialize in downsizing, senior moves, sorting household contents, and the like.

To find a daily money manager while you're alive (and who would, therefore, be well-positioned upon your death to assist with the administration of your estate), go to the website for the American Association of Daily Money Managers (AADMM) at AADMM.com.

If you would like an excellent (and concise) overview of charitable giving in your lifetime and after death, I recommend Arlene Cogen's book "Give to Live" (also by Niche Pressworks). The author summarizes different strategies to allow even people of modest means to leave a financial legacy that reflects their values.

Have ten minutes and want the thrill of searching for buried treasure? Go to MissingMoney.com or Unclaimed.org. Pour yourself a goblet of wine and search for every relative whose name you can recall. You may find unclaimed assets that you can rightfully claim yourself, or you may make a friend for life by notifying someone else about their own lost assets.

# LET LEGACY ESTATE ORGANIZING HELP YOU!

## Visit LegacyEstateOrganizing.com to:

- Join my mailing list and become a Member (don't worry, I will never sell my list).

- View my online "It'll make a nice sandwich!" tutorials.

- Schedule a complimentary Discovery Call to discuss your loved one's estate.

- Sign up for a 90-day Virtual Package to use me as your offsite, affordable "estate whisperer."

*Legacy* Estate Organizing LLC

# ABOUT THE AUTHOR

Eileen Moynahan enjoyed a long career with the federal government as an intelligence analyst working international criminal investigations before relinquishing her biweekly paycheck (and three-hour daily commute) to open Legacy Estate Organizing, LLC in 2016. A boutique estate administration business, Legacy Estate Organizing serves as a partner to the executor responsible for their loved one's estate (and their estate attorney).

Eileen's intent is to comply with both the spirit *and* the letter of the deceased's will or trust. Eileen also uses her business as a platform to educate others about the need for both quality estate planning (before death) and compassionate, efficient estate administration (after death).

Eileen provides concierge services to her local clients as well as virtual services to clients outside of her geographic region. She offers a wide range of service levels, depending on the degree of support that a client needs. Check out the helpful information on her website, in her monthly newsletters, and through her (unintentionally comedic) educational tutorials.

Please visit Eileen's website at LegacyEstateOrganizing.com for more information and to learn about her services. She can be reached directly at Eileen@LegacyEstateOrganizing.com. Eileen currently resides in Rockland County, New York, with her husband Ed Diaz … and someday a dog.

CPSIA information can be obtained
at www.ICGtesting.com
Printed in the USA
FSHW010955120219
55606FS

9 781946 533425